Shaggy Banks

Shaggy Banks

POSTHUMOUS POEMS

**Julia Watson Rhines
Steptoe Barbour**

Great Reads Books

Published by Great Reads Books
P. O. Box 2112
Bellaire, TX 77402
http://www.greatreadsbooks.com

Copyright © 2016 by John Rhines, Jamilla Rhines Lankford, Jesse Rhines, Jennifer Barbour Butler

All rights reserved. No part of this book may be reproduced or transmitted in any form or by any means, electronic or mechanical, including photocopying, recording, or by any information storage and retrieval system, without the written permission of the Publisher, except where permitted by law.

ISBN 0-9718694-4-8
LCCN : 2009936351
Manufactured in the United States of America

In loving memory of
Julia Marie Watson,
who grew up to become a poet,
and our mother …

Table of Contents

Preface i

Samplings

    Summer Song for America 1
    Alien Places 2
    My Crowd 3
    A Man of No Account 4
    Blood 7
    Christmas Bittersweet 9
    Ode to Egomania 10
    Dawnsight 11
    Deprived, We Adults Grope 12
    Now that Man Has Gained The Moon 13
    Paying Dues 14
    Bless All The Little Coffee Shops 15
    Shallow Thoughts 16
    The Half Daft Girl 17

Politics & Revolutions

    A Silliness of Politicians and Militants 20
    A Time of Dishonor 21
    Diplomatic Topography 24
    Children Want Everything They See 25
    Play Washington 26
    The Assassins 27
    The Heroic People of Prague 28
    The Sentry 32

Humor & Conundrums

    The Womanly Quality 44
    A Scientific Condition with God on My Three Sides 45
    A Vicarious Position Deplored 46
    Death Wish 47
    Go Forth in Preparedness 48
    A Sad Little Story 50
    A Sad Little Story Made Glad 51
    Doug's Trouble 54
    Had My Mother Ruled the Tribe 55

Harvard Yard Blues   *56*
The Solution to All the Problems of Mankind   *57*

Autobiographical
I Remember New England   *60*
N Street   *61*
Colored Studies   *63*
7th Grade Algebra   *65*
Library Experience   *67*
My Father   *69*
Ballad of a Stylish Rebel   *71*
Some Danced Minuets   *75*
Wrong Gods   *80*
Expatriate in Harlem   *82*
I Never Knew Sistuhs   *112*

Humankind
Drawing of the Line   *115*
The Showoff   *116*
The Underdog Champion   *117*
Trophies   *118*
If I Had A Sum Comparable   *119*
Barren Fruit   *120*
The Greatest Show of All   *121*

Travels Abroad
Dreamflight   *123*
Rain on a Swan   *124*
The Villagers of Mont Blanc   *125*
Ruminations on the Quai du Mont Blanc   *126*

Family
Funk, Junk and Me   *128*
For My Son's Admiral   *131*
Jesse's Poem   *133*
To Veronica   *135*
Alongside Jeela   *136*
Sisterhood   *137*
Apologies to Mother on Her Birthday   *139*
The Ones Who Wait To Watch The Plane Rise   *140*
Tired Old Words   *142*

Africa

    African Wildlife   144
    The Poets of Africa   145
    Broken Thread   147

Love

    A Poem for Love   150
    Everyone Wants Something All His Own   151
    Fair Warning   152
    Lacking a Partner, Play the Game as One   153
    Red Light   154
    Love, Blame Me Not for Disserving Ways   155
    Love Memories and Silky Music   156
    Love Takes Me Up   157
    The Race of Love   158
    Tremors After Love Flown   159
    Wry Toast   160

Nature

    A Mistake in Judgment   162
    Capital Spring   163
    Dominance of the Seasons   164
    Eclipse   165
    Fall Leaves   166
    The Huntress   167
    Noon and Afternoon Into Night   168
    Order in the Jungle   169
    Ordinary Blues   170
    The Coyote's Lament   171
    The Natural Circumstance of Glory   172
    They Still Write of Snow And Rain   173
    Wild Grass   175

Self

    Everytime I'd Think a Poem   177
    Challenges, Set Aside   180
    The Natural Dancer   181
    No One Has Taken Me By the Hand   182
    If I Could Rake the Dreams I've Had   204
    Obsequies   185
    I'm Always Losing Things   186
    In Remembrance of a Best Friend   187

Time   *188*
Surrender to the Sun   *189*

Parenthood

Children, Anyone?   *191*
In a Clear Glass Bowl   *192*
Play on a Premise   *193*
Prayer for a Good Motherhood   *195*
What is Life   *196*
Hasty Conception   *197*

On Poetry

A Laudable Avoidable   *199*
A Poem for Poetry   *200*
If I Could Toss a Poem's Words Up   *204*
In Gropium, After W.S.   *205*
O Poet Tell Us, How Many Twists of Heart How Many Smiles   *206*
Poems Landing   *207*
Poser   *208*

Race

Aftermath of a Game   *210*
Where There Are No Strangers   *211*
73,000 Days to Breakthrough   *212*
Black Slave Girl's Lament   *214*
Danse Macabre   *216*
Dies Irae   *217*
He Died Not in a Slipshod Way   *219*
Perceptions   *222*
Song of the New Patriots   *223*
The Advantage   *224*
I Dreamed of Langston Hughes   *225*
Shaggy Banks   *228*

In Maturity

Circle Closing   *230*
A Scientific Analysis of Sex Offered for the Consideration of Ladies who Admit to the Age of Fifty   *231*
Just Passing Through Greatness   *233*
Leap for the Sun   *234*
Shining Ways   *235*
We Shall Bloom Again   *236*
The Arrival   *237*
The Lifetime Traveler   *238*

Inspired By Other Artists
    A Pique at Ogden Nash   *240*
    Keats Saw the Leaves   *241*
    Night Pleasures from a Stranger   *242*
    Not That You Would Give a Damn Robert Frost   *244*
    On Meeting A Great Poet   *240*
    Stevie's Eyes   *248*
    The Eye of Andrew Wyeth   *249*
    The Feeders   *253*
    The Wit and Manners of Mrs. Alice Roosevelt Longworth   *254*
    To Countee Cullen   *255*
    To Diana Ross   *256*
    To Miss Margaret   *258*
    Where Vincent Stood   *260*

Index of Poems

Preface

No doubt objectivity is impossible when offspring attempt to define the significance of the work of a parent, but for whom they would not be alive. As Mary Shelly said in her Preface to the *Volume of Posthumous Poems* of her husband, Percy Shelley, published in 1824, "a narration of the events of my husband's life would come more gracefully from other hands." We agree. Yet, like her, we have no choice and now "hasten to fulfill an important duty—that of giving the productions of a sublime genius to the world," ten years after the death of Julia Marie Watson Rhines Steptoe Barbour, our mother, whom we fervently loved.

That Julia Barbour was a genius was an opinion held by literary experts who read her poems or, more likely, heard her compelling recitations. Mrs. Barbour was twice invited to read in the The Folger Shakespeare Library's Evening Poetry Series, and once hosted their Midday Muse program. Twice she received a grant from the Washington, D.C. Commission on the Arts and Humanities to develop and present her program of poetry exposure in D.C. public schools. She also read at local coffee shops, colleges and universities, was written about in newspapers and interviewed on TV—in spite of never having published a book of poems.

Fearing her work would be lost forever, Paul Hayden, Consultant in Poetry to the Library of Congress, prevailed upon her to record there. Until now, *Julia Barbour reads her poetry at the Library of Congress (Mar-22-1978)*, has been the public's only access to her poems.

Julia Barbour's wonderful works have languished in dusty folders and boxes in what we her offspring referred to as "the back room" of her last home—a once-forbidding obstacle course stuffed to overflowing with full dressers, boxes piled on boxes, towers of books rising from the floor, overlaid by the odd parasol from Paris, a dusty Chinese umbrella, gifts to her from the world travels she inspired us to take. We located 147 of the poems that caused poetry lovers to shout bravas at her readings. They are published here in book form for the first time.

It is perhaps with some guilt that we report Julia Barbour was a woman possessed of multiple talents, all abandoned in favor of being our mother —until 1968, that is, the year Martin Luther King, Jr. and Robert Kennedy were assassinated. Struck, we believe, by the fragility and unfairness of life, Julia Barbour wrote her first poems. Some are priceless authentic commentary on the racial strife of that era. However, her poetry is, most of all, starkly humane—full of wry and often side-splitting humor, and beautiful or profound or heart-wrenching commentary, on the world, nature, and humankind itself, on relationships, parenthood, celebrity, politics, living and dying. In the process, it offers behind-the-scenes glimpses into ordinary and privileged lives from 1920's Harlem to 1990's Washington, D.C.

Born Julia Marie Watson on February 3, 1923 in New York city to Charles William Watson Jr. and Pauline Turner Gears, our mother was, via her father's family, the descendant of house slaves Jesse and Amanda James on the prosperous Breckenridge plantation, Grove Hill, in Fincastle Virginia. When slavery ended, they camped along the James River, took their surname from that body of water, and in 1867 bought property there. Twenty-one years later in 1888, one of their eight children, Lucy Mary, married and gave birth to our mother's father, Charles.

On the maternal side, our mother was a descendant of the Africans, Wampanoag Indians, and English who settled in Connecticut and Rhode Island. Secrecy still surrounds the racial mixing that occurred and records are scarce, but we know our grandmother, Pauline Turner Gears, was raised at Holy Providence in Cornwells Heights, PA, a now-defunct Catholic boarding school established for the racially-mixed offspring of elite New England families. She was the daughter of Elizabeth Brown Turner, who was Wampanoag, in whole or in part, and Thomas Church Gears, initially listed as "white" and born in "Rhode Island" on an 1800's New York census, though the W for "white" has been crossed out and replaced with "B," for black, suggesting a modern change. In our family, they are regarded as star-crossed lovers. The perhaps romanticized version of their story goes that Elizabeth and Thomas fell in love and married in secret but when his family learned Elizabeth wasn't white, they forced an end to the marriage. Their child Pauline—Julia's mother —was sent off to be raised at Holy Providence, leaving Elizabeth to die of a broken heart and Thomas to wander unhappily the rest of his life. Years later, Julia's two eldest sons would be sent to Holy Providence after the death of their father to be raised under the nuns' stern message of avoidance of sin.

We also know that our mother, Julia, lost her own mother early in life. During the brief interlude when Pauline was alive, our mother lived in Rhode Island and in New Rochelle, New York, a period touched on in the poem *I Remember New England.* The superior education at Holy Providence had prepared Pauline for what was then a privileged position —personal maid to a wealthy family —and in that role she applied for a passport to sail to England aboard the Aquitaine (spelled Acquitine on her passport) from New York's Pier 14 on April 14, 1926. Our mother was three years old at the time. Not long after, Pauline died and we've often heard the story of how, at the age of 5, our mother lovingly stroked Pauline's hair as she lay in her coffin in New Rochelle.

From there, Julia Watson's story moves to New York city. Her father, Charles Watson, aka "Buddy," was involved in the New York theater scene, appearing in the production, *Shuffle Along*, with the famed composer/pianist Fletcher Henderson. His mother, Lucy Mary James Watson, the daughter of slaves, was now a talented seamstress/designer who worked for the Ziegfeld Follies and at an exclusive dress shop on Fifth Avenue. His sister, Marie, owned a beauty shop that catered to working class clientele. When Pauline died, Charles took to the road as a traveling actor/musician, leaving Lucy Mary and Marie to raise our mother —and, much later, to help raise us as well. Charles also worked for the American Greeting Card company for a time as an illustrator.

The prologue of the epic poem, *Expatriate in Harlem*, describes our mother's exciting life in Harlem, New York with Lucy and Marie, before they moved to Washington, D.C. where we were all born.

What may not be apparent is that as the descendant of educated house slaves and literate New Englanders, Julia Barbour was born into what was the elite of colored society at the time—families whose economic ties to white society had long allowed them to prosper, in spite of slavery, racism and Jim Crow. Before the move to D.C., Marie, our mother's aunt, worked for and traveled with the famous operatic singer, Grace Moore. They'd met in Marie's beauty shop, where Marie deloused Grace Moore's hair and loaned her a fur for an audition. Subsequently, Grace hired Marie as her personal maid/traveling companion, the latter title applying when they were abroad and free of America's race restrictions, which Grace famously opposed. In the U.S., Grace referred to her light-skinned maid as "French" when she could, in order to protect them both.

The family moved to Washington, D. C. in the 1930's where Julia Barbour attended Armstrong Junior High School and Dunbar High School, both of which had received a boon in the form of its brilliant staff—teaching being one of the few professions open to talented blacks at that time. Dunbar turned out the famous Dr. Charles Drew, Senator Edward Brooke, Congresswoman Eleanor Holmes Norton and other future leaders.

Julia Watson Barbour was not one of them, but she could have been, perhaps should have been. Instead, at the age of 14, she met and fell in love with the scion of one of the most prominent black families (see *Some Danced Minuets*) in D.C. at the time, Jacinto Aneille Rhines. The youngest son of a well-known Nashville attorney who'd traveled the world—and the younger brother of John Turner Rhines, unofficially dubbed the "mayor" of D.C. and invited to the White House by Franklin Roosevelt—Jacinto fathered four of us, then tragically died of tuberculosis at the age of 30. Her second husband, Rexford G. Steptoe and her last husband, Delaware S. Barbour, both of whom she outlived, would father seven more of us.

Therefore, it's easy to argue that Julia Barbour never published because she was too busy being a mother, per the dictates of the Catholic Religion into which she was born and raised —the stern message of the nuns of Holy Providence drilled into her at a young age by Pauline. Or perhaps it's that she loved people and being face-to-face with them so much, as hinted at in the poem: *My Crowd*.

What we're sure of is that many of the talents possessed by our forbears, known and unknown, seemed to have flowered in our mother to an astonishing degree. As a result, we thought all moms sang *Un Bel Di* from Puccini's Madama Butterfly while they cooked the oatmeal. We thought all mothers jumped dramatically onto the living room couch, cackling scarily while enacting from memory the witches' scene from Shakespeare's *Macbeth*. We thought they all scrawled congratulatory cartoons worthy of The New Yorker (see illustration on page 26) on *A* papers from school before hanging them on the kitchen wall. We thought all wrote Op-Eds for the newspaper. We thought all were so physically beautiful that people stared at them, like we stared at her, mesmerized.

We cannot account for our mother's love for and keen observation of nature. She was city-born and city-bred. Before financial troubles seriously befell the family, we lived in a lovely home at 1001 Urell Place, Washington, D.C., where our mother kept a flower garden, roses climbing up a trellis against the back wall —not differently from other homes, though. Somewhere along the way, perhaps starting in New England, the sky itself, the clouds and rain worked themselves deeply into her psyche and her poems.

At the ballot box, Julia Barbour was a conservative, but a rank liberal in daily life. Many times in public, a homeless person would approach. She'd greet the misfortunate one by name, open her purse and offer money for a meal. For those with drug problems, she'd escort them to a cafeteria and buy the food herself. She'd often assist them with the rectification of some governmental slight, or listen to their tales of woe and give comfort. She nurtured many a lost or unloved child, helping and encouraging them to obtain an education. No fanfare. Her giving occurred in private, soul to soul.

Born into material comfort, taught piano and literature and dance and song, no one had expected Julia Marie Watson to be anything but a worthy husband's gifted wife and valued mother of his children, but when the loss of husband or home forced her to work, she did. Not until January of 2006 did she retire from Federal government employment, after 44 years of service. She died that December at the age of 83.

Life had made her no softie. We, her children, were as likely to call her "Mother" as "Ma," because she was equally forbidding and adored. Accounts of slave children sold, of lynchings, of racism, had survived in her down through the generations —along with all the tales of our forebears' victories. She came to know about poverty and death first hand, and factored their stark wisdom into her being. She saw the world's cruelty and called it what it was. She saw its splendor, too. Sometimes we called her *Ereshkigal*, (Sumerian Goddess of the Underworld), dramatically suffering as she struggled to give birth to people then to poems.

In many ways, Julia Marie Watson was as exquisitely inexplicable as the world she watched and tried to understand. Did she ever find answers? Her poem, *The Arrival*, makes us think she did.

Concerning the contents of this volume, we are instructed, again, by Mary Shelley, who wrote, "I frankly own that I have been more actuated by the fear lest any monument of his genius should escape me than the wish of presenting nothing but what was complete to the fastidious reader." Us, too. We've chosen to publish every poem we found, the perfect and the imperfect, the weighty and the light, and we hope to do the same with a future volume of the poems still remaining to be discovered.

Finally, a note to her: Dear Mother, you have failed in the parental ambition expressed in your poem entitled *What Is Life*. In our opinion, the worthiest survivor isn't one of us. It was you.

—Jamilla, Jenny, Jesse and John

SAMPLINGS

Summer Song for America

      I, the privileged onlooker,
on any perfect day in the host mid summer,
can be seen in a Capitol cafeteria or res-
taurant gazing into the eye of All America.

      I, the worried American onlooker,
having cried all winter long over the Eagle's
wounds and mourned the contamination of its
young, now sense the season's recoverance
and with the greatest pleasure proclaim that
this year's tourists aren't loud enough!

Roll the rug out for short, fat, thin, tall,
straight-haired, jerry-curled, curley, kinky,
permed, beaded, braided teenaged America.
Don't tell them "Hush!"

      I, the analytical American onlooker
urge them shout, stomp, be rough! Let the
world in on their exuberance—their solid
gold untimorous stuff!

      I, the proud American onlooker con-
jure up lush phrases to sing America's song;
while the Eagle soars high over plain fields
where the uncommon corn is sown.

1984

Alien Places

Forlorn is the seed blown to alien places;
    brushed down invisite paths,
    caught in insensate crevices.
A seed emptying in one long falsettoed song;
    august features ravaged,
    the fine edge dulled.

O wind, lift this seed! Lift it for the
    ministerings of its master,
    to correct a life turned travesty,
    to fan away rubble collected.

O wind, forlorn is the seed blown to alien places;
    twisting, turning,
    adjusting, adapting,
    permanent resident of
    no place called home.

                1979

My Crowd

I don't care
about money or fame.
I'm going to
say my poems,
anyway.   (<u>to be recited with</u>
I'm going to   <u>classic sass. foot</u>
say 'em long,   <u>stomping and hand</u>
going to   <u>clapping suggested</u>)
say 'em loud,
going to draw applause,
going to
draw a crowd.
I'm going to make the crowd laugh,
going to
make it cry.
I've got to start the heart,
before I
move the mind.
And any heart I've got
I'm lending out
free,
so we can have a good time.
My crowd
and me.

        February 3, 1978

A Man of No Account

It was déclassé to speak to him, when you were sober.
I did, once, out of plain Virginia-bred politeness.
You should have heard the sudden silence and seen
the eye all fixed in frozen stares
dead at me!

They were the regular weekend elite,
dressed to the nines, chatting,
standing around or elegantly leaning, getting their
fine black heads just teasingly "tore" on
Chivas Regal, Jack Daniels, Budweiser Beer, et cetera.

My escort came to my rescue.
In true Sir Walter Raleigh style—or as befitting
a descendent of the ritziest house niggers (which was even
better here)—he too smiled at the outcast behind the bar
and extending his hand proclaimed, "My Man!"

This recognition, coming from one whose father had
gone to Harvard, caused quite a settling down,
believe me. The low hum of conversation
resumed all around.

But my brain branches were caught in a tornado of
wayward thought: why shouldn't I speak to a
human being I'd seen a hundred times before?
What had he done wrong?

I asked my companion, "Why don't people speak to Prince?"

"Just drink your juice, doll," he whispered.

I smiled cute as I could, shrugged and said no more on
the subject. At that time I was not one bit
liberated; rather, was nauseatingly deferential to most
gentlemen because—to tell the truth—I was frightened out of my
simple wits by all men. Therefore, when instructed to

drink my juice I complied *tout de suite*
like the bidding had come from heaven.

But quietly I studied Prince.

The length of him, from sole to crown, must have been
six feet six or seven
Frontally viewed, his face seemed rather long
and narrow from chin to temple, then
spread wide, high and handsome
on his brow.

His profile was, indeed, fine—its nobleness climbing
from forehead to parietal rise set off by fullish lips
curving slightly downward, nose prominent and
bridgehigh.

His coloring was unusual—almost metallic; not
black, not really brown—dark bronze
you could call it, with an undercoat of gold,
toned down.

His clothes were plain—khaki and tieless with blue
oxford-cloth buttondown.

He filled orders for repeat rounds quickly
without an attitude of rushing
and met the usual half-drunken, nonsensical quips
with professional bartender grace
but I saw boredom flit among his forced
amusement and, yes, a wistful sadness even,
skip across his face.

I never saw him make a play for a girl
though I think he could have had decent pick, on the sly
of course, among this colored café-society elite. Still,
he didn't have the air of a man who preferred men
to women.

I had heard talk about his deficiencies:
  he didn't drink, didn't smoke,
  he didn't have a car—walked everywhere,
  he didn't have a home or fabulous apartment.
  They said he lived hand-to-mouth,
  taking jobs as bartender,
  living in rooms.

One day I saw him at the public library…in the music room,
with earphones on, listening to Respighi's
Pines of Rome, (I peeked)
and there was something by Vivaldi.

But his tastes were versatile.

I saw him again one day, at the library, loading up—
checking out a Charlie Parker album and one by
Tatum.

And he had some books: Maspero's *Dawn of Civilization*,
Dubois' *Black Reconstruction*, a couple by
Galbraith, a poetry album by Dylan Thomas and another
entitled *A Hand is on the Gate*.

But whatever Prince did it was NO-NEWS anybody wanted to hear.

Of his non-importance I was indeed convinced.
The only thing that kept ticking away in my brain was
if he was of no account—as he surely was—
then why had somebody somewhere ever
bothered to call him *Prince*?

Blood

Blood, has a disconcerting way
>of charging through the arteries of EV-erybody!
>And, when spilled along with groups of, say,
>Four or more, being damned hard to properly place!

>Not even the RED CROSS knows— *(unless right on site*
>*with their labels at the time of Letting, to*
>*quickly catch this impatient fluid)*—not even They[1]
>know, just whose blood is whose.

Blood composition can completely elude:
>it can be anemic, hemophilic, RH-factored, "Bad"
>or, if none of this is true—
>no matter how renowned or famed the vein
>it's never blue.

Blood, is a scourge peculiar and a lifetime horologe to women;
>An ignominious memory to American Blacks;
>An exciting ritualism to their African cousins;
>A way to even score;
>The reason we walk upright in peace
>And gaudily sprawl on the fields of war.

Blood, is what is ultimately shed in the shape of tears
>for erratic disdainful children
>as nearly saturated in this bitter wet, parent yet
>reroute it, molding a salty, turgid lump, a
>sadly fertile growth
>in the privacy of the throat.

---

1. A reference to the days when the RED CROSS policy excluded the blood of blacks from its banks.

Blood keeps its secrets well. Can you imagine it coagulating
   into little whorls of glee as its path of truth
   is modified and/or cleansed!   Ahhh,Ha!

   Content enough to be the body's silent accomplice
   in public deceptions,
Blood can be quite an honorable friend.

1975

Christmas Bittersweet

Each year I wait for Christmas
Like a child of three.
My heart hurdling in anticipation
Of wondrous things to hear and see.

I hear Santa's rooftop cry, *"On Dasher! On Dancer! On Prancer and Vixen!…"*
As his sleigh streaks
Through the glitter of my dreams.
I see people come running
To join in the fun and
Sing and dance around
The dazzling Christmas tree.

I see stacks of carefully-selected presents
All prettily wrapped
For me and you.

Each year I wait for Christmas
Like I believe it's true.

1990

Ode to Egomania

It's a small circumstance that I flatter the grass to leisure here
   and graciously accord my time
   to the shade of the willow tree.

I've noticed that my gaze stirs the stars to nervousness
   in the sky—I must dispatch a rocket thereby
   to settle the childish twitter
   (*twinkle, twinkle,* indeed!).

And I must remember to encourage the dawn blush on
   it's really not disturbing; in fact,
   I bid it enter to attend my awakening
   which should be
   an annual public event of great interest
   which I shall be glad to present, free.

And after my presence has sufficiently cleansed the environment
   I'll be quite ready for retirement to
   my summer home which I call
   "Heaven."

My demise should be splendid and exclusively attended
   and the worms should have a sumptuous feast off
   the grandeur interred that is
   —*Oh, damn it!*—
   me!

                1976 (Rev 1983)

Dawnsight

Nearby at Dawn
Just before the light
There is no color in my room
Things look black and white.
Nearby at Dawn
In the clutter of my room
Things are clearer now
Then they ever are at noon.

The lamp beside my bed,
Its milkwhite gleam folding into gray.
The colors flung across my dresser top
The pink and green China-born straw
Mementoed on my wall
The children's crayon and pencil scrawls
The painted splash of red roses in an amber bowl,
By me, become artfully molded coals
Just before the Dawn.

The silent pandemonium of magazines and papers
Spread across my bed,
Books piled high, hiking air
Revealing nothing blue or green or red…

And to think that every day
This phenomenon evolves
In the ending dark
Just before the Dawn;
Unnoticed before by me
Until just now,
This late
I see.

1978

Deprived, We Adults Grope

Deprived we adults grope without the child remindful
   of how it was
To laugh and play and cry in innocence,
To share our joy, to place our trust.
And empty is the human bin without the residue
Of lives long lived to gather in.
But *ah!* — life's noon, blaze forth!   Fire
To the utmost out busied loins
And when our sun-kissed deeds are done
We'll have the pearls of dawn
To muse upon, brushed
With the mellow beauty of an
Amethystine dusk:
The two extremes of life which
I suspect are
The very best
Of us.

1978

Now That Man Has Gained The Moon

    Now that man has gained the moon
  will he lose the sea?

      the wind?
the gentle sway of tree boughs in the sweet spring of an
April:

        the feel
    of mist on the skin?

     the thrill
  of seeing bodily sinew strain and sweat in earthly
contest?

         will the look
of human forms floating indefinite and thistlelike through
space … thrill us more?

Paying Dues

Mainly, I write—I live,
Outside myself.

Because, inside myself lies
something taut, aimed, and as lethal
as the bows of my ancestors.

I would—could have let go
knowing I know my target,
but the target ever moves—changes,
to something previously
unconsidered—overlooked.

At times I've been surprised
to see it feeding at my table,
grinning at my jokes,
delivering essential news.

I shrug—un-nonplussed,
having learned that targets are
seldom absolute.
One may never move within range
deserving of the shot…

And so, this is how
I pay my dues.

                May 26, 1985

Bless All the Little Coffee Shops

Bless all the little coffee shops,
    all the places where you go to stop
    the inner bleeding.

Bless all the movies you see that ease
    the pain of life's
    raw dealing.

And the restaurants, big and small, posh
    and not, where you swallow all
    your wounded feelings—
    bless them.

And bless all the caring strangers who
    stop to fill in the
    empty spaces of
    your aching heart.

        April 1986

Shallow Thoughts

Shallow thoughts kept him alive
Saved his face
Massaged his pride
Swathed his torso in bandage bright
Prescribed associates for position's sight
Bade him live so spectacularly
That not a friend in truth had he.

Then when trouble made him delve
For deeper thought to save himself
So immune his foolish head
At first attempt he fell down dead.

1975

The Half Daft Girl

There she goes,
the half-daft girl
In her mother's place,
Now easing the burden of her father's
Marching age.

See how she carries his tray
Places his napkin
Fetches his water
And parts the meat from his
Chicken bone.

Not so daft for this,
When mother was alive
This child was an embarrassment at home,
Where she only stayed to sleep.

We watched her womanhood come alive in
The city streets and marveled
At how she avoided
The treachery of strangers.

Her parents, well-dressed and handsome,
Would pass her by, unrecognizing,
Sitting at a distance,
The half-daft girl likewise would look aside—
Never intruding on the privacy of their
Public world.

Surely her mother cried and wondered
Before she died what would become
Of this daughter and her dad, but

There she goes,
The half-daft girl,
At ease in her mother's place;
Her dad slowly following at ease behind.

She stops to wait for him.
He takes her hand.
Her face breaks in a loving smile.
No doubt she's amply fit for this; why, this is
Her time to shine.

9/90

POLITICS & REVOLUTIONS

A Silliness of Politicians and Militants

                    A silliness of politicians and militants
          is telling what they'll not reveal
      and exactly why they'll not reveal it
and how it won't be said.

It's bad enough to be hanged by the neck
        but why by the tongue as well?

                            I'd be surprised to find
                            more necks than tongues
                            pointing the path to Hell!

A Time of Dishonor[2]
—the best time to repent

And we are here on a darkling plain
Swept with confused alarms of struggle and flight,
Where ignorant armies clash by night.
                    Dover Beach, by Matthew Arnold

    The snow lies high tonight.
    I know not where the moon is;
    I have not looked out my window
    Nor have I consulted an almanac.

    In England, the cliffs stand.
    And her grievously tested people
    Prepare to bear a piddling plight.

    In Africa, starvation thrives.
    Vying only with disorder for attention.
    And the land—that land,
    World furbisher—world designer,
    With motherly tenderness and understanding
    fields her marrow.

    And everywhere,
    World leaders exchange cultures gracefully, swap jokes
    And raise their cups in toast to
    Cold war wives and mistresses while behind
    Carefully shaded eyes each calculates the cost of war
    Then quickly dismisses it in deference
    To visions of glories to come
    With the next slaughter.

---

2. Written during the Watergate Crisis, which resulted in President Richard Nixon's resignation in lieu of facing an impeachment vote in the House of Representatives. The following year, American troops were withdrawn from Viet Nam.

And in our houses,
In our American houses lights are dimmed.
Still, we see enough to negotiate heinous private crimes—
To fill new veins with death—
<u>Appassionato!</u>
To see to do in the dark of night
What jumps hideous
By the light of day—to see
Only what is soothing
To the eye

And in our land—
In our paradoxically humane land
Vexation spreads,
As in our Capital head after head appears
On the spikes of
Calvert Street Bridge.

And in a Great House—
In the corridors of this Great House
Walks a harried man—
His Lieutenant fled.
Just one of many who followed him not
So much in loyalty as to
Serve his own turn instead,
And this one too,
In dishonor exited.

And the chosen one stands—
Apparently steady;
Any reeling not readily
Discernible.
And if this boils the bile, O citizens,

Did we not demand pander to an odious mystique?[3]

---

3. "A Nixon campaign advisor in 1968 says, "…he could come up with clichés, and they all had to do with law and order." Nixon wooed white southern voters…[and] got the crucial support of Strom Thurmond…with promises to use a light presidential touch on enforcing school desegregation."— American RadioWorks, Campaign 58 by Stephen Smith and Kate Ellis

A pander spread thick
On a threadbare carpet of law and order? —
<u>What deception this!</u> to pretend
Easy commitment to the control of human beings
Held slave one day—free
The next!

Ah—Was not the wreck imminent!
Was not the scene laid upon that infamous carpet? !
That carpet—
Worn even more to a steamy rage
Where homegrown goblins leaped again
In jig-a-jag jublication to our peculiar
Fetish of Prejudice.

1974

Diplomatic Typography[4]

The Pyramids! The Pyramids!
We'd Supposed were where
Egypt is.
And until declared as
Flesh and bone
On view at Washington parties,
We didn't know
They'd left home!

1978

---

4. *The Washington Post*, December 21, 1977: "One of the guests within earshot of [Mr Hamilton Jordan, a top White House aide] said that shortly after the wife of Ambassador Ashraf Ghorbal, of Egypt, was seated beside him, Mr. Jordan reached towards her elasticized bodice and said something about wanting to "see the pyramids."

Children Want Everything They See

Momma, Momma, please buy me that
What?
I want an Angela Davis[5] Flag
And an Angela Davis hat
And buy me an Angela Davis Doll
And a tee-shirt
And some Angela Davis jeans
Aw, Ma, Sis wants everything she sees
Please, can I have some fun?
Can I have an Angela Davis gun?
Aw, boy, that gun's not for men
That's for girls
To give to their
    boyfriends.
Oh, look Momma!— There's an Angela Davis wig
Now wait you two —
Do you think I have a bank up my sleeve?
Oh, but Momma, here's the best part
You just wait and see
One day I'm gonna be real smart
I'm gonna grow up to be just like Angela Davis
Then they'll make a toy out of me.

1973

---

5. Angela Davis, a former professor of philosophy at UCLA and associate of the Black Panthers, joined the Communist Party following Martin Luther King's assassination and ran for Vice President in 1980 and 1984. Her large Afro hairdo became a trend-setter in the early '70s during her arrest, trial and acquittal on murder, kidnapping and conspiracy charges.

Play Washington

Oh it's lovely here on the bandwagon!
Where else would you have me ride?
Over there on top—
                of that tired old cart—
                        where I might fall off and
                                  bruise my hide?
    I simply love it on top of the bandwagon.
  It's like being a perennial groom or bride.
And I can be seen
doing the popular thing
while the rip-off goes on
  down inside!

1983

The Assassins

Here   There   Or just around.
Sitting on a stool in a place where
the hamburgers are forty-three cents
and the cheeseburgers fifty   and the turnovers
too sweet but cheap. In line at a movie,
on time   usually   with the rent Spent
from a night of asserting themselves with
waitresses…   As commonplace as
these words describing   Except
for a nearly imperceptible body stiffening
and a fiery glint espied
under a swift uplift of eye   at mention
of anything political
or at sight   of a parade
passing by.

1974

The Heroic People of Prague[6]

I

A thought is not more devastating set to paper than
  carried in the mind of man.
Janitorize it
Relegate it to the docks
Stamp it unfit for fit society
Encourage offended nostrils
  sniff
Fifty-six choruses of publicized disdain
  the thought remains.

And being not restricted to thalamic thinking
Inevitably beats through to the chairman brain
  and out to hit the air
  hear its whir?
It just bounced off the tip of Bila Hora[7]

How mad they be in Prague
  to think that thought
Forced to physical labor or idleness stops.
Did it not sprint the points of waves to come to us…to me?
  Incredible.
It passed by me just enough
  I'd say just enough
To not pass me by

---

6. "I read an article in *The Atlantic Monthly* in December, 1973, written by Trudy Ruman and it was about conditions in Prague and it sort of touched me as I think it would have anyone who has literary aspirations. A passage of the article, which I have here, reads, 'A new and more subtle kind of purge has been going on for the last four years. The oppression is directed at the Czech intelligentsia. Many have been forced to take manual jobs. Libraries have been gutted—."from the CD, *Julia Watson Barbour reads her poetry at the Library of Congress*, March 22, 1978; The Library of Congress, Motion Picture, Broadcast and Recorded Sound Division, National Audiovisual Conservation Center.

7. The name was intelligible on the CD. Bila Hora is substitute.

Just enough
To shutterize my ears
Flute the roots of my hair
        and notify my fears.

II

Yes, I read about it
It was advertised,
The purge in Prague
Like an eccentric fellow citizen long gone to explore foreign repertoire
   it has returned to greet me
This time to come to my side,
To my position, which is just to the
   side of an American inner city
Where life is reputedly and repeatedly
   so forlorn
One scare has time or interest
To pursue other people's purges
   so tense we lie, alert,
      in a constant state of gracement for our own.

III

But in Prague, my American complainants
A whole lot is going on.
For instance, a sociology professor
   washes floors
An editor makes sure store windows are squeaky clean
A playwright
   wheels dead bodies to the morgue—
(duties, I might say, not totally unrelated to former occupation)
And Eva, a former respected professor
   now waits on factory workers
She serves them beer and sausages on their morning break.
No mention is made of Eva's fare
that is, whether she herself eats or drinks too much
Eva declares that working at the lowest level

bears certain compensations
No demands are made of her.
And American lawyers, heed
Several Czech contemporaries work
   as clerks.

IV

The most reckless paradox is the lure government
   sets for writers
It beckons them with publication
   Most have declined ...*Ho, ho!*
Perhaps the most propitious line is cast for poets
   Most have declined *Ahhhh!*
Is it not revealing that a nation's most valued progeny
   in time of purge may be its poets.
For poets, heretofore content to pace through clouds,
Or expound the nightly machinations of water fowls,
   Ruat caelum, during perilous hours are
   known to heave thunderbolts
Without notice they rise
Sudden ramrod lovers of the native land
   Ecce pro aris et focis
Plaguing societal farce
Relentlessly pursuing the truth
Uprooting it when found
They proceed though ill at east and wary
   Undeterred by threat
   Undeterred by lack of honorarium.

V

Oh, the durability of intellectuals any and anywhere, anytime
   Prepares a tearful gathering in my heart
Cheers, Cheers! to you in Prague
   I know your kind
From mysterious Africa, pre-Babylonia and Mesopotamia
Before Egypt, before the Bible brought the tale of Genesis
   I know your kind
From the first intellectuals who sent their ideas and messages on the

wind
   and inscripted records on rock and bark of tree
   and left bits of insignia on the seas
   and erected sand
   to tell the story.
And if late-comers make naught of it or misinterpret it, too bad
Let them be compelled to make mistakes all their own

VI

You heroic ones of Prague
Even if, at this time,
   you lie laundered in your own blood
Know that your thought processes
   have been
   will be
Spun off into the air from the Baltic sea
   dipped in the Rhine
Whipped around the Alps
And pushed on through the Channel
Out to the Atlantic
To laze on down the Mississippi to
   curl up on that bloodied Delta, with our own
Before moving on to TOLL! TOLL! TOLL!
in a sound loud enough
   to bring down the world.

The Sentry

Prologue

Time: Night, Day, or Morning. Anytime. Anyplace in America.

Action: Three people walk together casually from back of stage, as up an incline, then down. Dressed in business, leisure and formal attire, they reveal no particular status but appear as common people engaged in the common pursuits of work, rest, and social obligation. Reaching front center stage they begin to speak.

All: We, the common people, are as sentries.

1st Speaker:
 We oversee our lives through the lives of those we choose to lead us.

2nd Speaker:
 We know the ones we choose to lead us are uncommon, So, bear watching.

3rd Speaker:
 In this, we, the common people, have a grave responsibility.

All: Aware of such grave responsibility, we, the common people, wish to, as far as possible, avoid it.

1st Speaker:
 We know what we want.

2nd Speaker:
 We know how much we can tolerate.

3rd Speaker:
 But, in our wisdom, we do not discuss this openly.

All: For one of us might become known as the one who started something. (warily)

1st Speaker:
    Then we could not move about freely—

2nd Speaker:
    We would spoil our delicious anonymity.

3rd Speaker:
    And we, the common people, merely wish to be comfortable—

All: But more than anything else, we wish to be left alone.

1st Speaker:
    Therefore, we, the common people, like hot-nosed hounds seek out our leader.

2nd Speaker:
    And present him, the Laurel.

3rd Speaker:
    Not because we are weak and he is strong—

All: Oh no—but because being prey to narcissism, all leaders are willing to, risk their lives.

1st Speaker:
    And in this, we, the common people, most ably—assist them.

2nd Speaker:
    We offer praise, applause, and a cornucopia splendiferous!

3rd Speaker:
    Which are all the more priceless because they are also, highly perishable.

All: And our leader looks at us, his followers, at first with <u>thankfulness</u>, and even kindness—until, he begins to see us at—

1st Speaker: A distance, and becomes—

2nd Speaker: transformed – surmising that what he sees is, witlessness—

3rd Speaker: a perfectly natural <u>cringe</u>, before the scene of his superiority!

All: How wrong in this our leaders be!

1st Speaker: But we don't mind—

2nd Speaker: No. We laugh—

3rd Speaker: Secretly.

All: With one eye shut and one eye open we follow our leader along his path of promises of good things to be.
(pace quickens)

1st Speaker: Even being amenable to change—

2nd Speaker: If such occurs—

All: We, the common people, are not to be made the fools for long!—there <u>are</u> limitations!

1st
Speaker:
>For, as we follow our leader along his path of promises of good things to be we grow—

2nd
Speaker:
>sensitive to turns onto dangerous highways;

3rd
Speaker:
>And when time comes for an accounting—we are capable—

All: Of demand!

1st
Speaker:
>By <u>force</u>!

2nd
Speaker:
>If need be. (parenthetically menacing)

3rd
Speaker:
>Ex<u>pose</u> him!

All: Make a writing example—a screaming warning to all aspirants to the God-Quality, <u>How</u>, <u>Dare</u> <u>he</u>!

1st
Speaker:
>In the end, we, the common people, make the decision: <u>Kill</u> <u>him</u>!
>>(flings this last at the audience turning away from
>>>his companions with authority)

2nd
Speaker:
>(Cautiously)   We can redeem ourselves by extracting the most worthy of his pronouncements, and call him—

3rd
Speaker:
>Martyr.

All: Meanwhile: <u>Kill</u> <u>him</u>!   There <u>are</u>   other Christs!

End of Prologue

—A Drama in One Act—

A sound of moaning.

Stage is dark, except for a light flickering on the body of a man tied upside-down on a cross. His torn clothes reveal his beaten mutilated body.[8]

Enter The Sentry.

Ignoring his charge, the Sentry walks band and forth, his rifle on his shoulder. He stops, stands at rest, yawns, stretches, scratches himself. He takes out a cigar. After savoring it—exploring it appreciatively with his fingers, he lights the cigar; standing spread-eagled he puffs away in contentment. The moans grow louder. There is a low gagging sound. The Sentry pays no attention. One particularly agonized scream causes him to whip around, and in exasperation he lashes out at the hanging man:

> Well, when you accepted the responsibility,
> you should have foreseen the possibility of
> one day hanging upside down in the <u>square</u>!   (affectedly)

A scream is cut short by a spasm of the man's body which shakes the wooden cross

> Hey!—Hey You! ...

---

8. Suggested by the death of Fascist dictator, Benito Mussolini who in 1945 was shot, beaten, and hung upside down in a public square beside his mistress for abuse by an enraged public.

Sentry hastens over to the body, straightens cross then shines his flashlight on the top where feet are tied. With the flashlight he scans the body until the light hits the man's face. The eyes are open and bulging, the lips trembling, and into the opened mouth fall drops of blood which the tongue is still able to sweep out onto the cheeks. After peering into the ace of the doomed man the Sentry suddenly recoils.

    My God, buddy!—it's—it's really <u>you</u>, eh?

The Sentry steps back in disbelief, semi-circles the man then walks away shaking
his head. He repeats this action several times flashing his light on the body as though to convince himself.

    Well, wh'd'ya know!
    Uh, uh boy!—I could have told you so
    You could have stayed like me, free!—well,
    As free as a man ought to be.

Moaning continues, but is softer. Sentry muses.

    There we were. Remember? Picking our teeth,
    Well, you never did that, but
    There we were, enjoying life together.
    We did an honest day's work
    For a pretty fair pay
    And after that, we went home and read in the papers
    What the world had done that day.
    And got in a damned good game of golf to boot, some weekends, I'd say.

    I was like you
    And you was like me,
    Or so I thought until—Hey! (Sentry had moved closer to the body)

    Watch that blood, buddy—
    It's the wife, you know,
    I'd never be able to explain <u>that</u> stain— (The Sentry laughs at his own joke)

    Who-ooo!—Yep! (Musing again)

I remember you <u>did</u>
Have a kind of funny way about you, at times.
A little restless, with a far-away look
In your eyes.
And then you raised your hand that day
And you were nominated, then selected. And I said,
'look at ole buddy there' and I felt
Kind of proud, you know—
Knowing I knew the guy who dared, yeh.
I said to everybody—I said, 'I didn't know he had it in him'—
Which wasn't quite true, you know, because well—
I did know you had it—like
A lot of us got it, you know—if we'd only
Take the trouble…

Well, we all listened to you.
And what you promised to do for us
Sounded Ok, uh-huh
Sounded good.
But then, buddy, you changed.

You seemed to forget
Us ordinary folk.
Some people who helped you on your way say
You even forgot their names—yeh,
People like me, well I don't know we seemed like
Just a joke.
I never believed I though—that you changed, in fact,
I always took up for you,
Though even I noticed something different, but I said
'well, it's to be expected, you know,
Look at his position…' yeh.

            (The upside-down man gasps something that sounds like
            "please, please…here…" The Sentry goes up to the body,
            and kneels in order to place his ear near the quivering mouth)

Huh?—
What is it buddy, —
Aw yeh…

Naw, I don't have a thing to ease your pain—wait now!
My grandmother used to say (Sentry stands)
If something hurts you
Just take a deep breath
And hold it—
Until the pain goes away,
But maybe she was talking about
Headache—
And, doggone it! I just bet I'm thinking about
A chest x-ray! ...

      (Sentry doubles with laughter)

But in your case,
When your pain's gone, you— you
Won't be here to care—   (Sentry is slapping his thighs in laughter)
Either way!

      (Then, — as if realizing his poor joke, the Sentry stutters in
        embarrassment)

Uh—Ah, Oh...ummm, fella, I'm sorry,
Really, I am, ah
I didn't mean it like—like it sounded (and, he snorts awkwardly)

      (In a soothing tone the Sentry continues)

But I know where you went wrong.
You catered to them that had fat pockets, all right,
But skinny scruples.
You sold your character, your integrity—you know,
Like they say:
You sold your soul! to them—

Yes, you forgot—you forgot
The qualities of a <u>true</u> ruler

      (The Sentry nods his head in knowing manner,
        walking back and forth. When he speaks it is in the voice
        of an orator—his stentorian tones are akin to those of
        a learned man)

A true ruler
Is the epitome of his people
A true ruler
Is merely
A higher representative of what they
Want to be
A true ruler
Is his peoples' High Priest! of moral order
And points of harmony:
He's bold in war
But cautious and shrewd in council.
He disdains the non-genuine
And he is careful of his associates—
A true ruler
Never casts his lot with Swine!
He is exemplary in everyday life
And the good of the people, is uppermost in his mind.

Yeh.
I admit
I read that in a book—Oh yeh—
You never knew I liked to read…well, I do
I used to sneak off with a book every once in a while
I'll confess. but I was never one for
Taking the lead—maybe, ah—if
You had read some of the books…

        (Sentry shakes his head, yawns, paces…)

        (The Sentry's interest seems, suddenly, elsewhere.
        Oblivious to the groans of varying intensity from the
        Upside-down man he goes over to a tree stump, leans
        on one leg and looks at his watch, then gazes off into
        the horizon)

Well, buddy,
My time is up.

        (Sentry turns and walks back toward body)

Boy! that's sure some puddle of blood!

        (Hanging man begins to cough)

Hey!—you getting a little cough there? …
Let me see if I have some
Lozenges…
        (Sentry rummages his pockets)

Naw…
I don't have a'one

        (Sentry now seats himself on the tree stump. He looks
         perplexed at the body, placing his chin in one hand.
         The body had quieted. Sentry looks around, and looks
         at his watch, like he is expecting someone)

Well.
I'm sure not working overtime!

        (A kind of gurgling sound emits from the body)
Uh… say, buddy—
You're…
You're dying, kind of—of slow—
If, if…I was you… I'd—I'd try to
Hurry it up.
You see, this next Watch don't know you like I do.
And he's a right mean, dumb young pup…
        (The Sentry rises, stretches and looks at the sky)
See—it's almost Dawn.
        (For the first time, the Sentry looks with compassion at
         the dying man)
I'd—I'd really,
I'd like to stay with you buddy—
Until you're
Gone.

        (The Sentry walks to body, examines it)

It looks to me like
You're almost through

And it is really getting late.

>(Sentry begins pacing, now rather sorrowfully: he looks at the man, turns away rubbing his chin and shaking his head, taking on a truly forlorn stance. He walks back to the dying man)

I wish I could <u>do</u> something—
Just—just for old time's sake!

>(He kneels on one leg by the side of the body laying his rifle on the ground)

But I can tell you this much—   (Sentry points to opposite exit)

They got another one out there—
Almost ready to take your place.

>(Applause is heard from exit, and over it a booming voice is saying: "My fellow countrymen… My fellow countrymen…" Applause finally stops: "Thank you for your confidence.")

Well, buddy, I gotta go.

>(The Sentry rises and walks quickly toward the exit, then out; then, as quickly pokes his head back in with a wave of his hand)

I'll tell the wife and kids you said
<u>Hello</u>!

The End

1973

HUMOR AND CONUNDRUMS

The Womanly Quality[9]

Yes, I, a woman
    am equal to man. I too
    have a brain that can devise
    any kind of inane or sane thing
    that he can.

The record will show
    I can plot and can plan.
    And I can shout loud
    with stentorian power enough to cower
    a mountain lion, I'm
    the new thing.

I am through
    surrendering my pride—my
    self-respect—to supply mere bodily needs
    but now mean to stand free
    for more purposeful, prodigious
    deeds.

I will show
    I can march in war, détente,
    mud or flood; and I shall
    equally step every day
    of the year; nary a cramp,
    nor female trouble,
    nor nervous disturbance
    shall curtail my will.

    All I need is an equal chance
    and a pill.

9. Rifling through papers in response to a request to read this: "I can't find it. This is terrible. You can't imagine what it took to get here *laughter*. I almost didn't make it. What did you do with "The Womanly Quality," Jamie? [daughter] Wait a minute. Honestly, this is too much *laughter*. [Recites another poem, "Time," still searching, then mid-poem lifts "The Womanly Quality" high, *laughter*] ."—Julia Barbour, The Potter's House, Washington, D.C. a reading in the 1970's

A Scientific Condition with God on my Three Sides

My condition is quite Isostatic I'd say.
In whatever direction I turn
I'm urged to go the other way, and
When I attempt to comply, why

I'm stopped on the other side!
The only remedy for this rejection
Is to assume a position of
Circumflexion,
Which,

Of course,
Couldn't be precarious *more!*
Because,
I could easily wind up
On the floor!

From which I could

(unless otherwise) rise
To be perpendicular   (not,
Mind you, parallel!)
Affixed in equal parts
Proximitous
To Heaven and
To Hell!

1975

A Vicarious Position Deplored

Of course, no one *wants* to die
but to my mind it seems decidedly wrong
and inordinately selfish—
when one has lived a full span of life—not
to relinquish one's place
to the young.

Replacing one's ailing parts with bits and pieces
of some other person is exceptionally
vulgar and particularly reprehensible if
the he or she alive were
nobody reputable.

Nobody one would ever invite
to one's barbecue, or

contrive to be indiscreet with,
or even notice on the street.
Indeed, being caught in the population census along with such a one
smacks of a dirty trick!

No, even the promise of the First Woman Presidency
couldn't persuade me to accept graft at all
though I might well become President
vicariously, if
someone
has
my
gall.

1982

Death Wish

Take care not of my looks when I am dead
Of beauty I will have no more need
Waste no money on a fancy coffin
A plywood box will do instead

Let my hearse be a truck by Hertz
Driven fast by my first-born son
If he's not available
Then anyone inclined and able
If I've a husband, let him be the one

And by my head lay a few of the
world's best books
In deference to my sole earthly greed
For far worse than death is the disaster
of being caught in the hereafter
Without something good to read.

Go Forth in Preparedness

Roy Slade has been appointed director of the Corcoran Gallery of Art...Slade has been acting...since Dec., 1, when the board in effect dismissed the gallery's two top officers...as a result of a fist fight they had at a Corcoran opening in November.
  The Evening Star and Daily News
  Washington, D.C., June 28, 1973

It was the Art Show of the year!—
A brilliant affair.
And anybody aspiring to an ounce of importance
Would have preferred death to
   Not being there.

The show was designed to give the world of Art a new lease on life
And every illusion that danced in an Artist's mind
Was on display
   That night.

Everything done in oil, watercolor, crayon, pencil, pen
(and some say Mud), was being represented
One Artist, inspired, he said, by
The Emperor's New Clothes
Thought the best way to present his painting was
   Not to paint it.

And, of course, there were those who thought the best thing to
Do with paint was, simply, sling it.

In any case,
Everyone turned to applaud the Curator and his Deputy as they descended
The Gallery's palatial stair, when suddenly—
These two gentlemen turned to eye one another with
Steady, deadly glare! And would you believe it,
The Curator gave to his Deputy
A hearty, backhand swipe! Blood

Pushed
Down the front of the Deputy's stock! But he
Retaliated with all his might!
And they locked in a furious struggle
Which straggled into the room marked,
> *The Future of Art in Civilized Western Life.*

Well!—
The horrified spectators ran for exits
And to the Gallery's upper floors.
Some prominent but indiscreet onlooker
Ran to call the law!
But when the policemen came
The fight was over and was explained as merely a little
> Cultural strife;

However, one distinguished black gentleman,
A friend of the Curator's, and
Knowing a bit more about the vici-situdes of life
> Whispered,

"My heavens, dear boy,
Had I known you were *that* piqued,
I would have offered you
> My knife!"

I

A Sad Little Story[10]

In the kingdom of the Fishes
a Shark and a Minnow mated.
'Twas from the start ill fated.
The Shark knew he hadn't ought to
but the conniving little Minnow caught his eye
by pretending she
was drowning.

Now the Shark, as large as he was, was
not too smart; thus, couldn't resist
so charming a dart aimed
at his protective instincts, so
he married her.

Little Ms. Minnow Shark, now married,
grew and grew with pregnancy
but found she was near incapable of carrying
her darling Shark's huge progeny, and he,
proud potential Papa Shark, was dumbfounded
and Oh! so sad of heart
when the day his Minnow's time was by
she verily split apart!

1973

---

10. "I wrote 'A Sad Story' trilogy … The first one is 'A Sad Little Story.' The second one is 'A Sad Little Story Made Glad,' and the last one is 'The Saddest Story of All.' I haven't been able to write that. It's probably out of date by now" laughter. ."—Julia Barbour, The Potter's House, Washington, D.C. a reading in the 1970's

II

A Sad Little Story Made Glad

In the Kingdom of the birds
a fresh little chicken heard
about a brave but discontented Eagle
so set about making ultra-sexy scratching sounds
designed to bring this noble bird down
and thereby improve her own social status,

And he, peeved with his steady
because she dared fly higher than he, reasoned,
"What I need is a chick with both feet on the
ground who'll be nesting in the hay
ready to make eggs when I come around."

So, for a while he came to visit
this cute little chick in her own backyard
but he soon grew bored and thought, "this
is really too provincial." And having
read Shaw's *Pygmalion* several times
began to entertain grand designs
so suggest to this chick that they
fly up to his apartment which was high
on the mountaintop but she, being
not so dumb, knew how to stay with an
advantage therefore claimed she'd gladly do it
if she could, but she
simply wasn't up to it.

The great Eagle was befuddled, betwixt and between
so decided to implement an old regime;
he'd fix this little chick: he'd impregnate
and marry her.
She had long given her pills to her friend

the little red hen so
this idea appealed to her.

Well the Egg she laid almost started an earthquake.
It fell like a bomb; fine feathered friends
came from miles around to see the new-born son
who was a sight to see. Not only
did not an Eagle eye have he
but his wing span, though impressively expansive,
gratuitously swept everybody in the barnyard
under its protection
which is not where everybody in the barnyard
really wanted to be.

Not only that, being so well equipped for
leaving the ground,
you would think that this ChickEagle
would have loved flying around
but it was inhibited, so
just went peck, peck, pecking.

The poor parents, being responsible in the
best tradition of their kind,
tried to shield the product
of their misalliance
from the taunts and jeers
of its more identifiable peers,
but to no avail, so were glad for the day
a famous doctor came their way,
took one look and said,
"Why, I can use *that* in my book,"
And their child happily resides
in the care of the great
Dr. Seuss.

Royalties aside, the mother cried
(and any mother would)
and Papa Eagle flew down often
to soothe her
until one day he came

and found things not the same
because his little chick had run off
with a guy named
Rooster.

The Great Eagle sighed for he had long realized
his mistake.

Finally, he took as his new bride his old flame
the lovely lady Eagle.
He had overcome his male-Eagle
chauvinistic pride
and now allowed his bride to soar as high
as her beautiful wings would carry her.

And there they sit regally today
in their plexi-glass mountain nest
sipping Irish Tea and listening
to the sounds of Leonard Bernstein
and now and then she reads to him
from a little book titled,
"All About Genetics."

1973

Doug's Trouble

Doug was a young colored fellow
who vowed he'd marry no other
than a white girl with blue eyes and long silken hair
of yellow.
(When he was small Doug's mother often read him the
story
of *Rapunzel*)

At last he met her, and she introduced him to
her brother,
whose skin was whiter, whose eyes were bluer, whose hair
was longer,
silkier and yellower than her's was.
Poor Doug was befuddled.

Then came the solution to the problem: the girl
declined marriage in line with the objections of
her mother.
Her brother said, to comfort Doug:

"Believe me, you won't miss her…
Anyway, didn't you know you aren't supposed to
marry my sister?

But since white skin, blue eyes and long yellow hair is
your thing, Doug,
don't grumble, there are others.

See? I got back the ring.
Nobody ever said you couldn't marry
her brother."

Had My Mother Ruled the Tribe

Had my mother ruled the tribe,
ruled by a wise hand the tribe would have been,
but my father did.
The hand he raised in rule was mainly strong.

Harvard Yard Blues

I've ridden a horse from F.A.O. Schwarz
And sung a Puccini aria
read Dickens, Orwell And Franz Werfel
But I've never read
    At Harvard.

I've played Rachmaninoff
And been in love
And felt the pangs of love unrequited
Am fat, was thin,
But to Harvard I've never been
    Invited.

I've planned and won a case in court
And lost my children to their father.
But won the fight to own my goat
And when my house burned down
Saved two kids, one coat
But am unvalidated
    by Harvard.

I'm a fair poet, so it's been said.
Sans Harvard, it must be arguable.
But look at Whitman, Poe, Emily D. And Ali,
The last of whom opted for
    Oxford!

Some say I've done well in this earthly life
Some say I'll be at my best afterward.
But lo! the stone shall shout behind my head,
"At Harvard, she wasn't acceptable!"

1982

The Solution to All the Problems of Mankind

Separation is the answer   Apartness
is the key

                           Once we secede from each other
                           the better off we'll be.

Intellectuals in one State   One's inferiors in another.

                         Murderers shall control a State
                         Reserved exclusively for Mothers.

Women past thirty
(with IQ's over eighty)
must be exposed.
Give them the shaky State of California
{or the iceberg tip at Nome (Alaska).} or make a pact with Rome

                         Thieves as usual will be protected
                   And so that rejection they shan't feel
                     Shall be allowed to proceed as usual
                       And keep any State they can steal.

Fertile men and women will be collected
in a State selected to contain
equipment made to see to it
this never happens again.

All of which is just a start toward complete release of States for
   the inhabitation of those who please the least:

Babies, children, teenagers, young adults, middle-agers,
senior citizens, old people, and people-in-general.

Warmongers and Peacemakers
Athletes
Non-whites, non-blacks, others

Protestants, Catholics, Moslems, Jews, Infidels, Heretics, others
Heterosexuals, Homosexuals, Bi-sexuals, and others
Lawbreakers, Lawmakers, and Law-observers
Surplus Populations, the Police and dissident Nuns and Priests…

After these are all properly separated the rest of us (at last!)
can live in peace.

                1973 (rev. 1982)

AUTOBIOGRAPHICAL

I Remember New England

I remember New England
And the snap of birches burdened under ice loads
And my tobogganing days
When I fell warm and laughing
Into my blanket of snow.

I remember New England
And the dependable, dry smiles of kindly disposed
Neighbors and the honesty—as
Intrinsic a part of the scene as
Crisp cold and log fires.

I remember New England
And the tinkle of a small, silver bell calling me
To meals served by a servant
I dared not call kinsman,
And Aunt Kate taking her place
As helmsmistress
Of our austere table.[11]

I remember New England
And whitefaced playmates and the emphasis on
Sparse speech and manners,
And my beloved mother's soft
Leavetaking of life.

I remember New England
And how my heart's gone unmended ever since.

---

11. 200 Overlook Circle, New Rochelle (Pelham), NY, in the mid-to-late 1920's.

N Street

At 4th and N, in Washington, D.C.: a brick's throw (depending on the arm) from Dunbar High School, the alma mater of the Distinguished Senator from Massachusetts, Edward W. Brooke.

They say it's hell living in a black ghetto
But when you're a retired bootlegger's little niece,
It can be sweet.
That's the way it was on
N Street.

"Papa" they called her uncle,
Although his name was John.
Big and Tall and Rosycheeked, he put on
A fancy way of living few black men, or white then
Could meet. He was the king on
N Street.

Storekeeper, Doctor-next-door, Pharmacist on the corner—
They could only hope
For the respect shown Papa.
He was best friends with the police inspector
Who told his cops they damned-sight better know
How to act to Papa whenever they saw him
Off or on
N Street.

And Papa was a humanitarian:
He fed the poor.
And gave his shell-shocked brother, Elgin,
A sandwich, fifty cents and a jigger of gin
Whenever Elgin
Went around to the back door
Like he was supposed to—
And would have given him more
Had Elgin not called him vile names plainly heard
By everybody on
N Street

Papa's little niece in her Paris-made organdy
With matching parasol watched
One hot day
As he picked up pieces of shimmering meat
That had been hacked
Out of old-man Mundy
And told Admiral Richard E. Byrd,
(Who did it),
After all it was Sunday
And Papa liked things neat on
N Street.

And Papa couldn't write his name
But could draw pictures
And did same
In his little niece's books.
This got him one of her
Downcast looks.
He'd try to make it up
By allowing his wife (his niece's blood aunt)
To give children's parties,
Which were always
Terribly unique
Because nobody went to parties on
N Street.

Just Papa's old bootlegging friends
Somewhat slowed in step
But still
Quick with their hands,
Were always dropping in.
Papa's little niece played classic piano
Other than that
She was shy
Fragile
And structured narrow.
She felt
Intimidated
Even in his Pierce-Arrow.
She had certain reservations about Papa and
N Street.

Colored Studies[12]

As majored in in Washington, D. C., in the '30's, when the word "Negro" was used only by historians and the uncouth and black was respectable only at funerals

Injustice was all around and I knew it
    I spied Despair lurking
        In all the corners of our lives
    On the Hill.[13]

But we splendidly pretended
    And deftly sidestepped and evaded
        The garbage thrown
            From the white side to our own.
                                      And sometimes
                                      We ate it.

But every now and then I'd snatch off my blinkers,
    Throw down my shield!
        And divest myself of my cloak of lies
            And I'd go below Florida Avenue, or across town to
                Wherever they, the subsocial and poorer others,
lived
                In those tucked-away courts and sidestreets.

And I'd jump a frenzied doubledutch, play Red Light, Birds Fly
    And scream!—
        And run up and down the Alleys
            And on the Playgrounds
                Test my girlish athletic prowess,
                                Like I had
                                Never been allowed.

And then one day a very black,

12. Published "GW Forum," v. 5, No. 1, Winter, 1975, a journal of opinion, for The George Washington University by the Faculty Senate..
13. "The Hill" one of the four residential areas of Washington, D.C.'s black upper class community.

    Short-haired, "but smart"
        Girl I admired
            Came home with me
                From my nobody streets.

I brought her home for my benumbed, lightskinned,
    Trying-to-be-right family to meet
        And they hated me for it
            And so did all the color and residence—right
            Friends
            I never had had anyway
                                    And finally,
                                    So Did she.

7TH GRADE ALGEBRA[14]

Lord knows I tried to keep my legs together
in 7th grade algebra
like grandmother said
all girls should do
(not only in 7th-grade algebra, she
said, but outside too).

But a charismatic teacher
or a particularly difficult test
can cause a girl to thoughtlessly
become too rapt in class.

And I, an especially attentive type,
At just such times as these
Tended inadvertently to
Drift apart at the knees.

Though mesmeric the sight
to the boys in my room
twas a chafing enigma to me
since under my dress
was nothing at all of
sex allure to me.

Snuggies? – overlaid with
blue-ribboned drawers
worn by a medal-winning lass
whose idea of sex
was practice track at dawn!

How I longed to be like Aslee
who sat up front
in the row next to mine.
She was the perfect lady
eminently successful in keeping
her skirt, legs, and knees in line.

---

14. "My physicist friend, Alan, wants me to read this." — Julia Barbour, The Potter's House, Washington, D.C. a reading in the 1970's

I continued to tug and pull, miserably
trying to thwart these crusty boys
in this inane thing they would do
when one day, to my chagrin and dismay,
I espied Aslee looking too.

1990

Library Experience

The day I received my card to the children's library
  a group of yellow-haired girls was in line.
We exchanged 3rd grade unpleasantries until
  my turn came to sign.
This card was my greatest pride. It
provided me with lovely friends of diverse nationality
  and degree (at the time people
  were one and the same to me), then
  my favorite playmate <u>The Little Match Girl</u>
  died. It

wasn't her fault!—
She simply froze in a doorway
  having struck the last of her matches for warmth.
She'd been told not to come home until she'd sold
  all her matches that piercing cold Nordic Christmas night
I was heartbroken. Aghast,
  at the cruelty of her father.
  (It never occurred to me she was white.)

The <u>Twelve Dancing Princesses</u>! (Even
  then I was cosmopolitan in choice of friends.)
I didn't see they weren't like me
  for I was surely like they as we
  danced the nights away-

And O what fun <u>Under the Lilac Tree</u>
  (Miss Alcott let us play),
Beth, Jo, Peter and Wendy, and Alice
  (though some of her friends were hard to know)
Tom Sawyer, Huck, Rapunzel, Black Sambo
and me.

Prince Charming?—
I assumed there'd be one for me like
  for the yellow-haired girls.
Weren't our library cards the same?
In the years that passed I found I was
  far more fortunate than they.
By then I'd obtained my adult library card
  and learned why my prince
    never came.

My Father

My father never saw enough of me
(in my opinion)

And I?

I saw him,
a creamy-brown/beige, yellow-ruddy clay
God delineation of the Male
privileged to live a man's life
In any guise he chose.

A splendid chanticleer my father was—
a lion only a fly would dare come near,
A man whose bold hold on his breathing space
chilled the spine of fear

And drew
pretty, flirty ladybirds of varied hue,
And piously particular ones too
to dance and preen and pine within
His charged wake of true love
that would never be.

On this yearning gallery
my father aimed his spray of sugar words,
And trained his beam of constant attention
to bathe and finally beckon
the lucky ones into his enchanted house
of temporal warmth and ardor.

Soon enough he'd tire
and end it all with a brutally abrupt
Stroke of his artist's brush,
a decisive take-up of his writer's pen,
A concentration on his fighter's fists,
An expert flurry of drummer's sticks,
A swift and final drawing-on of his
handsewn dancer's shoes.

> The lovely ladybirds would fly away,
> sent in heartrendingly crippled flight,
> And one or two sang no more songs
> for my father, or,
> For that matter, for
>
>   anybody else.

Ballad
Of A Stylish Rebel

Aw gee, when Jay's old man kicked him out the house
    for neither working nor going to classes
        and Jay's books, and prints of de Kooning And Klee
    and his African batiks
           and Jazz albums
            and collegiate artifacts and
        Ivy-type casuals came sailing out behind
    and his Mother stood weeping
        with her long hair let down
            and Mrs. Neal across the street
            retrieved
      Julien Benda's "The Betrayal Of The Intellectuals"
just minutes before
    it went down
        the sewer
  we were glad we were around
            to view it, Man
    because it was *pro*found
    and
    sig-ni-fi-*cant!*

And we all looked after Jay.
    fellows and girls, hiding pieces of his belongings in
        our houses
  pridefully lending out our basements
      after midnight
  and feeding Tim's Famous Hot Dogs and Pickle Chowder
      with Macaroni salad
        or french fries on the side
      and sneaking cold cuts and even
        some of Mom's cherry pie and milk
  to our own biggest rebel.

When Jay raised, quite possibly the first
        black
        fist!

                    to the sky we *thrilled*
                and gave each other knowing
            cohortive looks
                    and our conspiratorial little hearts beat
    run-away rrhump-rrhump-rrhumps
                            in anticipation, because
                JE-sus!
        this was *it!*

We followed Jay to 19th And T
            where the meanest, drinkingest, non-employedest misfits
                you would ever see
    hung out   (nobody knew where anybody lived).

                        and Jay hung burlap
                        and melted colored candles
                        all over his wine
                        and RC cola bottles and
                            burned incense
                        or lit up the place with
                            his own hand-rolled cigs
                while moving his head in time to
        Roach,
            and Clifford,
            and Sonnys' Rollins And Stitt,
                and Bud, and Miles, and Monk, and MJQ,
            and Trane,
        and Arts Blakey and Tatum
                    and Brubeck and Gerry Mulligan and Chet
    and Birdsounds
                and the place would be crowded with aficionados
                    just coming and going in silence or joining
                in moving their heads and matching MAX on drums
with
        their hands
            beating
                time
                    on tables, backs of chairs, and milk cartons,
                and there was little notice
                        of sex

                    although Jay did take a chick in.

Jay wrote book reviews for the Saturday Review, he said,
          and articles for the quarterlys, none of which we tried to
                understand much,
                    or even ever saw, as I recall,
            but he did verbalize magnificent
and when he painted his outside door purple with pink dots and orange,
        yellow and green stripes, we all knew
                          it was pro*found* and very
          sig-nificant!

Once or twice in the bank downtown
I saw Jay standing at attention cap in hand
dressed like a schoolboy in his corduroy
replete with knit tie
        while his mother wrote a check.

                      But we never paid attention to
            things like that
because,
        Jay would be back expounding politically on quote,
          "the situation" unquote, and
              theorizing economics
            and passing out histories
          in attempts to jar our
        capitalist inclinations:
all of which was mostly lost in the sound of Miles's horn and the crunch
    of potato chips.

                  one day Jay's father
                  followed his Mother to
                  the bank after which came
                  a long session with hunger
                  then Jay got a job. we were
                  appalled at this—we felt be-
                  trayed and cheated
                  but relieved and exhilarated at
                  reports of how jay treated it.

And when
>he got fired we celebrated
>for three weeks straight and
>when Jay got put out for non-payment of rent
>>we sympathized until our partying funds ran out
>then went back home to self-righteously tell the story to
our parents or argue about it with
>disapproving husbands and wives.

Added to his misfortunes Jay's doting grandmother in Virginia
>died.

>>Ten Or Fifteen years hence I happened to be
>passing through Virginia
and met Jay: he had become a local Federal government official,
>with a neat house (his grandmother's, of course)
>a wife, two kids, and
>>I couldn't believe it—a monogrammed screen!
>>this screen protected his very traditional
>front door, and remembering his
>>>drop-out stance
>>I thought WoW!
>this is really really pro-found
>and very, ve-ry, very
significant!

>1974

Some Danced Minuets

A delineation of the native colored
upper class quality in the Nation's
Capital, before 1954

1

Well, yes: you could say they were a special class.

Surely the women held up their end of pretend and doggedly ignored "never was."

> Their speech was soft and fine, their manners flawless.
> And in summer
> their daughters carried parasols
> and worse pastel eyelet, voile, dotted swiss and dimity
> dresses or plain linen ones
> and pongee won a special deference.
> Their shoes were of genuine patent leather
> or calfskin—plain and expensive. And their hair
> softly curled around the contours of
> delicately-tinged faces.
>
> Their soft-bodied sons were compelled to excel
> in every discipline, except
> athletics.
>
> And their homes were superbly imitative of
> the easy aplomb associated with
>   Angle-Saxon gentility and taste.

2

Yes, I admit, they did jealously guard their group.
Oh such menacing airs and graces!
> *(Princess Grace, as daughter of a bricklayer, would never*
> *have been accepted without her Prince!)*

What? Ridiculous, you say. Of course.
But they were aware—painfully aware of their
descendancy from slaves   (from master too).
But they never tolerated belittlers.
Their aspect set barriers, giving instant warning to
all so inclined:
>	*We don't need your reminders.*
>	*We know who and what we are.*
>	*What uplifting thing can <u>you</u> contribute?—*
>		*leave as legacy?*
>	*What can you be that will raise the level*
>		*of the group?*
>	*Don't bring complaints or fuss.*
>	*We're sorry prejudice is hampering you.*
>	*We prefer ignoring it. So please,*
>		*stay away!*
>	*Don't hamper us!*

Yet the least rise in the community,
by whomever,
was applauded. Rumor sped out,
Notice was posted by
community press,
Minor celebration went on
in places
totally unrelated.

    3

Yes, admittedly, color could get you in.
But the *open sesame* was achievement, chiefly.

You see, color was the refuge, I think—yes, yes,
a refuge.

I say let them who can find refuge in
time of need, take it—Of course,
take it.
Wouldn't you?
God knows they needed it; for despised they knew
themselves to be
on both sides.

No. I can't say they didn't enjoy their little coves of
color prejudice.
But in them they built platforms
and prepared emissaries.
For the truth was, they welcomed
any of whatever color
who held like ambition
and commitment.

Because,
a peculiar competence was required:

the ability to sit alone and fearlessly among
the opposition,
chatting amiably while
manipulating canapés and tea,
and simultaneously memorize
all slips of the tongue,
all attitudes and nuances,
and, when employed propitiously,
the contents of the files.

    4

You're right—they did keep themselves apart.
But should they not be called blameless in this?
The choice, after all was clear: life or death.

I insist: they were not heartless.
Bad news brought unforgettable sorrow and an uncommon
communion—public lynchings, burnings, whippings,
the inhuman segregation that left stricken members
dying by roadsides...

    Roadside Death Interlude
        (sung in a blues tempo)
  Oh Miss Juliette Derricotte
  We shan't forget your dying caught
  unattended
  On a pinetree-lined southern road.

Oh lovely Dean of Women at Fisk
Why weren't you taught the risk
of auto wrecks
In the land where no Hippocratean oath
Was honor-owed
To the luck of dusky folk.

Likewise Miss Smith
Born beauteous Bessie
We know you didn't mean
To get that messy
And let your bluesy blood stream away
To death
All along a lonesome southern road...
Oh no....

Oh beautiful ladies
How the honeysuckle cried
To see you die so.

Oh beautiful ladies
How the honeysuckle cried
To see you die.

And each little daisy
Wiped a tear
From its yellow eye ...

Wiped a tear
From its yellow eye ...

...its yellow eye

5

Ah! How such tragedies clouded their eyes with rage!
Even while they sniffed in disdain.
Rage!—Rage! stiffened them.

Rage, missed with bewilderment at such cruelty—
turned somehow, someway, to a new final
resolution.

And so they suffered,
alongwith and side-by-side their darker brethren
and withstood it all.

Their minds became crowded storehouses of this hideous, lurid
memorabilia.

But some of inconsequential passion, endowed
neither with valor nor understanding
remained safe
behind the fringe
in a lifestyle of cringe.

And some sprang forth on errands of lawful (and unlawful)
rectification.

But all departed their houses each day to preach,
teach, advise,
doctor,
defend,
inspire,
to rally,
to bury…

*and to emblazon the despicable insignia upon our memories
and fire our minds! and, well—
Yes …
some danced Minuets.*

1982

Wrong Gods

I prayed and prayed and prayed.
At night, I got down on my knees and begged
To see my brash, my strong, my handsome Dad and
MaMa surely reassured me, so that
On the appointed days
My heart rose in my throat and
Stayed and stayed and stayed
And eagerness skipped around inside me
But he never came.

I made my First Communion,
Was Confirmed and taught Sunday School
And believed everything I'd read or heard about
God and Church and Good.
And when I married, instead of one God
I had two and I obeyed, obeyed,
obeyed.

Then my young God fell ill.

In my bewilderment I sought the third God in my trinity:
The Priest. He said, "Push death away, away
With prayer, regular attendance and repentance,
repentance, repentance."

So, even though my bin of sin was near empty then,
On Saturdays I sold my fantasies
To the Confessional, but felt no better;
For, all the while I admitted, *"Mea Culpa! Mea Culpa!*
Mea Maxima Culpa…" I knew
It was truly not!

Then my stricken spouse[15] took leave
Of this brutal earth, and the Priest soothed, "Have
Faith, faith, my child!" And I cried, "No! No!

[15] Jacinto Aneille Rhines, October 16, 1918-November 17, 1949

Never again! I'm too filled with doubt!'
I've found faith of no mortal use!—
When HIS luck runs out!"

1982

Expatriate In Harlem[16]
THE GOLD BUTTERFLY PROLOGUE

1.
Pete was my father's brother. His sister Ree
was, of course, my aunt.
Pete and Ree both knew
long before the NEW YORKER did,
that A. Philip Randolph was
mostly mouth,
and had it not been for his
good wife Lillian,
he would have ended up
   back down south.

2.
in 1929 when we were moving out
of the Dunbar apartments
Asa Philip Randolph had not yet
moved in. Ree was getting out,
she said, "before that
driftwood from the south with all
their kinfolk",
moved in.

---

16. "I was born in New York. [To Potter's House hostess:] Sorry, Dottie, but my grandmother's from Virginia *laughter*. It's [this poem is] a true thing. I'll tell you what happened. In the time when Adam Clayton Powell was brought back to New York to be buried, I went up there. I got involved in the funeral. I hadn't been to New York in so long and being in Washington where everyone lives so well, I was really unprepared for what had happened to Harlem. When I lived there in Harlem, we lived...I just can't tell you how well we lived—I don't know how or why—but we lived really well. My aunt had a manicurist come in every day...[This poem] has different sections... 'The Gold Butterfly Prologue' tells about when I lived there."—Julia Barbour, The Potter's House, Washington, D.C. a reading in the 1970's

3.
Ree said she was only thinking of me
    by moving to Washington, D.C.
    Old M Street High (renowned as
    DUNBAR) was her alma mater; therefore,
    she reasoned that a respectable
    education was obtainable
    only in the Capital of the Nation—
    in the more "salubrious climate"
    of an elitist segregation.

                                          4.

                              Pete didn't agree,
                      Neither did I. No matter: they
                      brought only a shell
                      to Washington, D. C., for if
                      anybody ever left a heart in any
                      place other than San Francisco,
                          it was surely me.

      5.
  My heart stayed behind, at random, on Sugar Hill,
Lenox & 7th Avenues, in the Railroad Flats—the
Brownstones, on the ice in Central Parks East
and West,
down at the battery—the bowery—over
on the East side,
    sitting on a curbstone on Park Avenue yelling
"Taxi!" when I was five and tired,
on the scenic railway at Coney Island,
eating Chestnuts,
riding the top deck of the Fifth Avenue bus and
    the EL—
my heart remained in New York City
where Pete and Ree and my mother and father lived
perhaps not wisely, but Oh My
did they live well.

6.
And in Harlem I danced the Charleston and
and the Black Bottom
to the tunes of a piano player named
Fletcher[17] who my daddy accompanied
on the drums.
    And I'd be so overcome
    by the rhythm
    that I'd squeal and Shimmy with 'em
    till I wet my bloomers behind
    the screen where I was hidden.

And Fletcher and daddy would stop
to go and get the mop
and was I thankful they never once
    told Pete And Ree.

7.
Because,
    it really wasn't considered proper
    for even little colored girls like me
    to dance the Charleston. And that Black Bottom
    was simply low and common and
    it was sluttish to even think of Shimmying
    or to wear "wrappers" or
    wear your galoshes open, but gee…
it sure was fun to me.

8.
And I remember Florence Mills
dancing nearly nude
around green satin pillows
on a stage. And I
gazed in stark amazement
at this black beauty
and exclaimed, "Oh look grandma, Florence Mills
is showing her boinky!"—and a

---

17. Drummer, pianist, composer, arranger, recording artist and band leader who helped develop the formula for Swing music, performed by big jazz bands.

white man in our box was so delighted
he gave me a five dollar bill and
a peppermint candy cane for each hand.

                                                                   9.

                  And there was the handsome black
                  Beau Brummell from Barbados—a
            Mr. Edward van der Cruyz his name was. And
              when that magnificent lifted
              a fragrant fingerbowl to his nose
              and sniffed it
              then its contents forthwith drank…
                  high-class colored hopes
                    sank.
          And when he went on to declare
              that glazed mandarin pear
                made him constipated…
        every male among 'em choked,
            and all the ladies pretended they'd fainted!

10.
And there as the elegant Brashear—the black satin
swedish trained masseuse
    who
had been awarded something
by the King. Indeed, he was much
admired by rich young and old white gentleladies
    for the ease,
    and comfort,
his expensive ministrations
could bring.

                                          11.
                  And in Harlem Ree had a
manicurist come in every day to do her pretty
nails. And I slept on hemstitched French
doublelength sheets, and I tried on Pete's
aigrettes and wore her money belt and dragged
<u>Lucien Lelong</u> beaded bags across the floor

>   having tucked high-priced
>   French aromas in back of my knees and behind
>   each innocent ear.

12.
And downtown I'd try on Grace Moore's[18]
 furs and her
   evening wraps
and sit entranced on top her grand piano
while she practiced operatic arias and the scales.

And I'd watch Irving Berlin smile with pleasure
when my Aunt Ree sang his <u>Blue Skies</u>, and his
<u>My Blue Heaven</u>, and we all cried
at the sadlovely way Ree sang
his <u>Always</u>.

>   13.
>   And sometimes on Vincent Youman's lap
>   I sat and made fun of Fanny Brice
>   behind her back and secretly thought
>   that "Auntie Grace" couldn't sing
>   much better than my Aunt Ree
>   and not nearly so well as Rosa Ponselle
>   whom she hated, though I wondered why
>   since Auntie Grace was really
>   much prettier.

>   14.
And I pranced around the deck of the Isle De France
until time came for Auntie Grace and Ree
to sail away.

>   15.
>   And I had white satin paper with gold-embossed butterflies
>   on my wall,

---

18. Operatic soprano nicknamed "The Tennessee Nightingale." who performed on Broadway in the 1920's and debuted at the Metropolitan Opera in 1928.

And Ree had pale blue with silver birds
in her room,
  And Pete had mauve with plum,
    And in the parlor and hallway was beige satin-striped silk
      and in D. C., all
        the gold butterflies were gone, and so
          was Harlem.

I.   HARLEM FIRST

    A.   <u>The Entering</u>:

Perhaps others have told it better—
Hughes, Baldwin, Claude Mckay…Garcia Lorca, but

I must tell my own tale
of HARLEM.

Entering off the George Washington bridge at
one-hundred and thirty-fifth
I thought we had missed the mark.

Shucks, I said, we've run into the city dump.

but no. it was truly
HARLEM.

And I was viewing no horror movie
where the creatures
walking upright were

unembalmed absentees from some
cemetery…NO,

they were the people of
HARLEM.

and I? …properly D.Ceeed, GSeee/ed, Nation's-Capital pressed and

processed, I

quite naturally flared my governmental nares, sniffed in disdain and privately exclaimed:

"Oh no...this can't be...I must go back! This is insane! I must leave this place...I ab/so/lutely   can/NOT stay!"

Then I looked again,   and again, sighed and

finally cried,

at the decay

that is

HARLEM.

B. Fitting Descriptions

HARLEM: the elephant graveyard of blacks in America.

HARLEM: an odious collage of trash in the streets,
rottening food,
rats and dead cats mashed
  like hamburger in the gutters.

HARLEM: counting the churches in every block you might think
that the eyes of the populace are bright
with the fervor of religion: (Oh, Yes Lord!) If
you didn't know
they were ablaze
with dope.

HARLEM: where......Yes I thank you...Despair is alive and doing well.

But so is strength. Hammered strength. Chisled-fine Despair.   Not a rare ingredient in black folk, HA! don't they sur/VIVE...Thrrr/IVe on <u>This</u>! ...grappling valiantly all the while with the spell/death feature of their existence...... they, they, THEY....

E$^a{}^t$ D$_E{}^A{}^T$H   a$\cdot$ $\cdot$L$\cdot$i v$_e$. ...$\cdot$ $\cdot\cdot$ $\cdot$ ...Ah, you s^{illi}f^y this pronouncement.
                                    eh! ....

                                                            Oblivious,
             to the scene before your eyes, you DE/NY the power of the HARLEM

      crowd   don't you???   DIS-believing, and scorn/ful of its blood strength.
                                  But allow me sketch Black Harlem's ancestral might
                             as journalized in the mystical diary of scarlet instances—
how out of the pestilence befallen glorious Africa, her coveted sons and daughters
                                                       like an ooze unstoppable
                                                            snatched death from
                                                         between spasms of the land
                                       fashioning a new JuJu. how they fed Death
               to the fishes of the middle passage, Wooed it in the virulent
         holds of the slave ships then took DEATH by the hand and led it
    to the sugarcane and tobacco acres, and to the cottonlands of the South,
                    and bade it fertilize southern fields,   then installed it as
     permanent guest hidden away in the bedchambers of the BIGHOUSE. And
                    while they suckled and simpered   and served the whines of those
           foolhardy enough to tag themselves,   "Master" and   "Mistress", they
                         left their small ones not unattended, BUT
                                       introduced them to DEATH and
       made the old tyrant play MAMMY/UNCLE   to   their young…

                     These DEATH-Nursed ones, in turn, sought sips of freedom
                         in the half-way place of HARLEM,   preferring the scarceness
                                       of tree/lined streets to those where
                                    mannerly blooms pop gently from boughs
                                             burdened by an iniquitous

remembrance.

                                    Therefore poetry lovers and lovers of all things
                       pure and beautiful   may you see that DEATH   to black
                                                folk
                                                            is no joke, but
                                                                 is REAL
                                                         and so familiar as
                                        not to be feared   but courted
                                                    exquisitely,
                                                               met fear/
                                                            lessly when required

                                    and always
                        to be respected.

   I saw a HARLEM FOLK deal with this
   Old bugger Death, on Easter Sunday
   Morning in
        Judah Church In Harlem.

C.   Judah Church In Harlem:

   1. The Congregation

                Death was sitting in a far pew
                    but not one member of the congregation
                    gave him so much as a
                    side view.

                Young girl ushers took their places,
                    efficient and crisp as fresh
                    lettuce leaves, in
                    their starched and spotless
                    white.

                Mature women entered queenly chapeauxed
                    in colorful hats and
                    elaborately wound turbans
                    which clearly overpowered
                    their lowly positions
                    in the "Misses Anns'" kitchens
                    from early morn to
                    late at night.

                Some men arrived meekly behind
                    major domo wives,
                    and some, eager and sunday-primed,
                    came to fling aside their
                    daily roles of
                    servility and
                    pose.

Children squirmed
> like nothing worse mattered
> than being indoors.

And the voices of the congregation,
> their matchless resonance
> a low thunder in unison
> with the choir,
> crescendos in the
> "Hallelujah: portion of
> Handel's glorious
> <u>Messiah</u>.

2. <u>A Most Unusual Preacher</u>

Then in strode the young minister.
One of many in Harlem
But this one was out of the ordinary,
Uncommonly unusual.
More famous he'd become
For lying across the steps of City Hall
Than for leading the people of Judah.
But with him they were in complete accord.

They knew he had not arrived in an El Dorado.
They knew he'd give no hint
Of a number to play.
They knew he had come to
Steer them through the days of Harlem.
They knew he had risen early and walked all the way.

He had prepared no text
Nor borrowed one.
Nor did he use the words of some legendary philosopher
Or rearrange those of the fashionable mouthpiece
Of the day.
This was a most unusual preacher.
He allowed his heart to have its say.

The Reverend Jehu Zehaniah Dorcas: an authoritarian
Figure radiating commitment,
Sprang to his pulpit.
Impressive at every flick of his robes,
His was no staged showmanship,
No pose.
The whole posture of the man discharged a fine
Courage and the revelation that
Here is a man to be counted on.

And as his sermon rolled across the congregation
The contained look of its ravaged features
Gave way to the Sunday-come resolution that
This week too shall pass away.

And you could see
Shoulders straighten
And dulled eyes catch fie
And you knew that this religion was serious business,
Not quite what "ole massa" had in mind.
He had tossed them a mighty rope
That they held with all their might
And as they toughened to it they grew into
A subdued race of giants.

3. <u>Congregational Mowdown</u>

The Easter Sunday congregation sang,
Clapped,
Prayed,
Testified
And strutted in march time
Up and down the aisles.
Then as one
They turned to that far pew in the corner
And looked death unswervingly
In the eye.

Death flushed,
Got up,
Drew tight
His voluminous cloak
And departed Judah.
After all—
He'd only stopped by,
For a little rest,
A little calm,
Before the heavy work
Awaiting him
In the deep, dark night
Of Harlem.

D. <u>View Of Lenox Avenue</u>

1. <u>Streetblight</u>

After church I stepped out into the Sunday air.
Pollution thick but no submissiveness there.
Not a trace of submissiveness in the faces of the
People of Harlem.
Disappointment? Yeh.
Waryness? Of course.
Ignorance? Of a kind.
Stupidity?
None.

walked on down Lenox Avenue:

I saw three tall men
    lingering in front of a shop.
    Identical in listless aspect and
    Identical in vanquished heart.

    Three tall walls with eyes only peering up,
    over and around
    the invective slung at them
    like lynching rope,
    by an Afro mother/daughter/sister/aunt:

"Ya'll get outa th'way Curtis—kindly let me
through. Since ya'll won't work nowhere, you can, at least,
move!

They obliged. I crossed to the other side of the street.

I saw a pretty little Hershey-colored girl of about eight,
   with great dark eyes,
   and a thick cord of frizzy hair
   hanging almost to her waist.
   She was laughing at the lewd showing by a scabby
   old man half-hidden in a doorway.
   he was offering her money
   to come up to his place.

I saw a boy of about twelve
   at curbside, sleepy-eyed, scratching
   absent-mindedly at his thighs

Rage and sudden grief
collided inside me. I stumbled,
then regained my pace and
continued my walk on down
Lenox Avenue.

2.   <u>Dreamscene</u>

Instead of seeing what I saw there
   I observed Impala leaping in the bushveld
   and a love affair between a Zulu lass and lad
   under the umbrella shade of an
   Acacia spread, "Ah, it must be a lucky blend" I
   thought, hearing soft, girlish sighs
   swinging on the high arcs of air…
   or so it seemed to me,
   listening there.

Self-soothingly I smiled, "That this is not HARLEM is obvious."
   Besides, sitting beneath a fig tree nearby
   I spied three tall men and I

lingered discreetly to watch and hear,
fascinated by their fast-paced conversation
and deft management of a pot-bellied calabash
which they passed among them
without a drop or splash of its
refreshing elixir of millet beer.

And I heard a young man say seductively to a young lady passing by:
"Why hello sweet sister. How about meeting me tonight
by the cocoanut palm down by the river?
I'll show you the moon, yellow as a
mango."

"Ha! More likely it'll be the mangrove swamp with you
foxy bro/thaaa," she laughed away, flashing her
pearly-toothed bravura—
Sassy—Female—and Free, in
Africa, or
so it seemed to me.

3. <u>Snapback</u>

I saw,
    a tall Rubens-proportioned lady
    with skin colored rich, molasses black.
    She nodded to me in greeting
    and I politely nodded back.

She was immaculate in
white-patterned blue
with ruffle slashed diagonally from
shoulder to hem.
The Sunday gentlemen gazed in admiration
But she took no notice of
them.

A large navy blue hat
dangled a lush pink silk peony; it was
a fit crown for her statuesqueness
swaying atop her high-piled hair.

She walked with such grace—
such poise—that you knew she had
forgotten it was there,
probably because it belonged to her
and was no "Miss Ann's"
cast-off affair. I thought;

Ah, beautiful Afro mother,
you are a fine example of prime
black stock and
would have cost several thousand pennies
down on that old auction block. For you,
many a planter would have sold his
favorite surrey and
placed his own grandmother
in hock.

A long, shiny car drove by slowly.
The lady continued walking. The
white driver called and beckoned then
took something from his pocket.
The lady hesitated,
stopped,
walked to the car,
talked.
The white driver opened the door, the
lady got in, they
drove off, and I
at last, seeing what I saw thought:
But this, then, is <u>real</u>!

II.   THE HONORABLE ADAM CLAYTON POWELL

  A.   <u>The Sagittarian Feature</u>:

Dipped in fire,
the arrow blazed
its brilliant trail   past   assenting heads
past mouths agape and   bowed in wonder   and past

                    an equal number of sodden eyes   cauterized   with
    hate.

                                        ...this arrow,   this splendid shaft,
                            forged Rococo,   streaked a glitterpath
                    tended by clusters of flittermoths   —preening
    —prancing   ever-ready with their portable Court   to pay tribute
            ephemeral   to whatever new grandeuw.   And, as usual,
                        such spangled wake drew   a few soberhopefuls who
    wished   only to bask in the warmth   and storeaway
                memories.

                            The Arch Bowman loved   the applause   as
                the string of his bow drove   his arrows   clean
    and true   through a target   struck honorable.

                            But public approval   as usual   stirred
                    a cunning competition.   Soon the conspirators
            knew the time had come   to lay plan   for fatal sin.   And,
    the flittermoths   dancing so near the arrowhead   foolishly aided
            in its poisoning.   And the Arch Bowman,   believing himself
            inviolable,   ignored the scum,   unaware   that allowed to
                    swim   on   top,   scum boils   a   deadly
            brew.

                                    It was too late when he knew.
                His arrows had become   detestable   and the target
        continually   moved out of range.   His arrows returned to pierce
    him through   and through,   but the old Archer stood his ground,
    craning his bloodied head   like the champion   he was   until he
            fell dead   in the arms of   a soberhopeful   who would long
                    have the warmth   to
    remember.

    B.   Press Conference At Abyssinian:

                The in-fighting was going on
                    between the Press and the Black Nationalists

in the outer rooms of Abyssinian
while church traditionalists
conducted the conference in firm, above-it-all
stance.

Remnants of old marchers-with-Powell,
constituents, and just plain
admirers of the Congress, parried sorrows
and just stood around.

Press Question: What do you think of the statement, "'King left many legacies, Powell none at all'"?

Abyssinian Response: "We, as black people, are demanding an apology from whomever made that statement. Reverend Powell's legacies are what you see in front of you. I am one." said the black VIP.

Press Question: "Do you admit that your minister did a lot of playing around?"

Black Nationalist Response: "Kick that white son of a bitch's <u>ass</u> outa here! Now! Much commotion, and scuffling sounds.

Abyssinian Response: "He may have played some, like many of his colleagues, but he made up for it when he sat down to work."

Press Statement: "It's been said that—I guess you know, that because of his color—some people have said that Reverend Powell really thought of himself as...as a white man... and he had a...a contempt for you up..."

Black Nationalist Interruption: "God Damn! I got to have me a piece of that m.........f.........g bastard!" Much commotion and scuffling sounds. It took several men to restrain the outraged spectator.

Abyssinian Response: I....I would rather not respond to that statement young man....but I will say....I must say that, if such rumor is circulating in your community it's only natural...and it's hostile propaganda even so…meant only to make black people distrustful of one another. It seldom works, however. (Applause). Yes, he could have passed…like many among you have done throughout this country's history, and are doing now. But Reverend Powell had no need for such deception. He was a black man proud to be a black man. His self respect would not have allowed him to hide behind a false set of credentials. Adam Clayton Powell was a man, sir. Not a coward! (Applause)

C. Some Private Ruminations:

>   I found my way into the main body of the church.
>   I was alone.
>   It was the first time I had set foot
>   inside Abyssinian.
>   Shivers of discovery raced through me
>   and my heart beat fast.
>
>   Besides, I expected Pete and Ree to
>   dispatch lightening bolts
>   after me because
>   they had been ardent anti-Baptists; also,
>   Abyssinian had supported the views
>   of A. Philip Randolph, "that
>   good-for-nothing from the south,"
>   which to my aunt Ree
>   was a position never to be
>   excused.
>
>   But there I stood—at his pulpit—admiring
>   the masterful design—the lovely
>   curve—which permitted each member of the congregation
>   "to see."
>
>   An unliberated thought flew free:
>
> >   …may had he had   just the right wife   say, like
> >   Lillian Randolph—   as wife

who could have understood
the importance
of his life,

and made it her business to...to <u>stay</u>—to stabilize
and supply a free-spirited,   generous, and
immovable
barricade...

I had ever met the Congressman, but had been close
several times...
he was usually occupied, as was I but each time—strangely—
his eyes, in scanning a room, caught
mine
and I would see—or thought I saw—
reflected in his eyes similar longings, disgusts,
and impatiences—or,
did I imagine it?

It came to be
that as he left a room
he'd turn and smile at me—we
never spoke, would simply
nod goodbye until wherever...
next time.

I think I first saw doom join
his entourage at a
café-society style affair
in Washington, D. C., but this time,

when he glanced around at me his countenance
bore the look of a magnificent, born-free animal
finally trapped, already lapsing into
a state of paralysis—
its carcass preparing the feast
upon which mites would feed—or,
did I imagine it?

Now standing at his pulpit, in his church, all
alone
I felt not out of place, somehow, only like
he would have smiled
had he known.

Someone walking in, "I've got a camera—
want your picture taken?"

I quickly waved the intruder aside.
Then, left in the privacy of my foolish notions,
Just like a woman,
I cried.

D. <u>One of the Six-thousand</u>:

    Naturally,
        everybody in HARLEM knew
        that Adam was coming home that day. Those of us
        who had gone to bed at all the night before
        had risen early.
        The day was gray.
        Snow was expected.
        It seemed that March had
        reined in its winds, had, indeed
        substituted a "little nip" which,
        in the case of Adam's coming
        was not inappropriate.

        The people in the place I visited were going crazy
        on the phones…
        "What th'hell do you mean? Damn right, they
        should pay for his transport!
        Right or wrong the man
         is a former member of the United States Congress!
        Fuck what he did, man! …
        he ain't the only one…"

They called City Hall
>and the power guns all over New York,
>and the White House, and
>finally Texas,
>where they said it was a "shame" and all, but
>Lyndon wasn't hone. They agreed
>that the Congressman's body should be returned in
>dignity like any other former…

>"Oh, No Indeed! …. Nobody could all the Congressman, common baggage, Oh no indeed…"

>We hung up, dejected, but feeling that
>had Lyndon not been in the hospital,
>he surely would have interceded,
>successfully.

I went down into the street
>and whom should I meet but one of the six-thousand—
>that famous lack 6,000 who had marched
>with Powell when he was a young, dedicated man of
>twenty-two—
>marched, against City Hall, a
><u>fait accompli</u>, nobody
>had ever accomplished before, and
>won—way back in
>1931.

>"He was a fighter, that Adam—
>I was on the front row then.
>At the end. And I'm
>going to be on the front row today
>when they roll his body down
>the plank of that airplane."

>"Do you have a ride?" I inquired.

>"Well, no—I don't, but the good Lord's
>on my side. He'll find me a way."

"You may ride with us," I volunteered, "If
you like."

"If I like?" he exclaimed. "God bless you child!—
and thank you!"

"Thank you, Jesus" I heard him whisper, as he
followed me inside.

Out of the corner of my eye I glanced up at the
sky. I

didn't know whether we had room

for this old guy.

Had I been used?

E. <u>Waiting for Flight 18.</u>

    1. <u>Stormy's Not Only Weather.</u>

       We knew that cars had long been lining up
           outside Abyssinian.

       We hoped we'd be on time.

       The old marcher of '31 urged our young
           preacher driver:

           "Don't spare the horses son.
           If you think you might run
           out of gas, here—take this
           five dollars and buy us
           some."

           "Aw, don't worry sir. That's all right,"
      the young preacher laugh, "If

anybody's entitled to ride
it's you, so just
sit tight."

A male black nationalist affixed a flag
    to our car. Being
    Mrs. Conservative from
    Washington, D.C., I winced,

"uh, my—that flag won't get us far."

But its flourish didn't slow or
    even put us on caution, so
    before we knew it—after
    a wild, terrifying ride over ice
    that almost slid us off into the Hudson—

we were there, at Kennedy Airport.

Adam's plane was due any minute.
    I used the time to observe
    his constituents,
    noting that though the wind
    was blowing up, bitter,
Stormy's not only weather:

    some people bit their fingers;
    some were cursing,
    some crying

    Some stood huddled in groups,
    praying or talking; and some,
    hoping that a personal acquaintance with
    the congressman showed,
    looked important;
    and some looked stoic:

    All looked forlorn,
    entrapped in the magic meaning of
    this moment.

2. <u>It's a Small Airport</u>

I was startled to see a profile I knew
cross the viewmaster of my past.
I scanned the back of familiar curves now all
padded in fat. And
the magnetic, mischievous wand of time
turned me and my old school chum
eye to eye:

"Fatima!" I cried.

"Julia Watson Rhines!" What are you doing
in New York chile?"

She flung out her arms
   I outstretched mine,
and the cold wind blew open our coats
   as we rushed to embrace.

She bowed her ice cold lips,
   I puckered mine.
But my aloof cheek deflected her slightly
   frozen kiss, taking it
   lightly on the side.

"Oh sweetie, this has wrecked me! Girl, I could
die! Adam was my <u>man</u>, the best. He really
was you know…I don't care what they
thought about him in D.C. …those folks
down there have always been unreal…girl you've
got to come and <u>see me</u>…"

Fatima was of course eulogizing politically.
   But she had always chased comets, rainbows, and
stars, as well as the boys in the bands
   that played the Howard Theater,
as I recall.

She had been every vaudevillian's bobby-soxed
　　delight,
our own little "groupie" far more sad
　　than strange,
and now, nearly forty years later,
　　she had not changed.

She still talked in dreams
　　about clubs and
fabulous scenes and glamorous things,
　　and dropped names.

And I remembered my long-ago pain
　　at her slights, her cuts and
condescending way
　　when she was young and pretty and popular—
when pretty I was too
　　but far too frightened and dumb
for it to matter much. My
　　single valid credential in our
exclusive high-school club
　　was my big house on The Hill.

And I fantasized how if now was then
　　how different we two
might have been, she and I,
　　each living at her
opposite pole, Fatima—
　　the fun loving, regal Leo, and I,
the unpredictable,
　　eccentric Aquarian.

And as we talked at the airport
of that wonder, wishful, idealistic past
when we had no inkling
　　our hopes were
bustable balloons, not meant
　　to last—I
never let on that I knew
her Utopia had crumbled, had, in act,
　　never been built.

And I at least wiped and eye when not long after
Reverend Powell's funeral I heard that
   Fatima was dead.

Meanwhile,
I understood when I phoned, at her invitation,
and found Fatima still not-at-home, to me—
even now, nearly
forty years later.

3.   <u>Here He Comes</u>!

    A voice yelled, "Hold on to your ears! Here he comes!"
        We held.

    Fatima, vigorously waving, crying out, "call me later!"
        was shuffled away into the crowd.
        I stepped back and around
        to move in,
        my camera clicking.

    The wind was blowing hard now.
    We could hear the big, high hum.
    Groups were jockeying for
    position, media people and photographers
        were on the run.

    Off the plane first, came
    Skip, the Congressman's son, then
        the King's last remaining
        Queen, his cherished,
        "Miss Darleen."

    The coffin careened a bit down the ramp, between
    some bold bags, GI canvas, and
        Samsonite.

    Someone murmured, "Will ya look at <u>that</u>! Jesus <u>Christ</u>!"

    The coffin was draped with the Stars and Stripes.

The black national group, solid
up front, determined,
   and looking mean,
broke through the police cordon, ripped
the American Flag off Adam's
coffin and replaced it with their own
   Red, Black and Green.

III. THE DAY OF THE FUNERAL

 A. <u>Tears, Miracles and Loving Recollections</u>:

 I could not stay.

  But on that day I witnessed the beauty
that is HARLEM.

  And I understood why Langston Hughes,
had stayed to draw
his portraits there.

  And I said Amen, to
HARLEM.

And on this day of mourning I saw miracles:

HARLEM, became almost sedate again. And clean…

  The trash collected itself
  and relaxed to slide
  out of sight into
  the sewer, or
  was zipped away on a
  quick blast of helpful wind.

  The rottening food became whole again,
  and wholesome, titillating indifferent nostrils
  and heretofore nonchalant salivary
  glands.

Previous apathetic viscera made tugging demands for
nourishment.

With appetites back, grocery stores that morning
buzzed
with more business as
usual.

Then expectancy hit! Word was passing in the old-fashioned way,
   of the Congressman's coming:

Old women stood in knots, shoulders shaking,
Old men straightened and stared ahead.
HARLEM'S addicted citizens with
their singular grace and fatal sensitivities,
   held private wakes in run-down
   bars along the route,
and in garbage-filled vestibules.

And those who could
were in full, cleaned-up sight
having made sure their high's were right
   so that no nods
   would bring embarrassment
to this most mournful occasion.

And some were remembering, speaking their grief
   out loud
   in the midst of this strangely silent
   crowd who full
   understood the need.

   "Adam cared," intoned one with ravaged face. He
   <u>cared!</u> …" the voice broke.

Silence.
   "And he never asked nothin' for ya, uh…uhhh."
Silence.
     "I'd be dead if it hadn't been for Reverend Powell"
       began another.

"Know what he did? He fed my whole family—my wife, my kids."

Silence.

A young woman turned and said "But that's a minister's job." (grumblings of disapproval heard)

The man shook his head, "hot what <u>he</u> did miss. That man helped me kick…that man's why I ain't a dope fiend today…sticking that shit…excuse me…that poison stuff, in my veins."

Amens heard.

"He stayed with me,"—the man continued, — "talked to me, and cleaned up my vomit…just me and him. In a room."

Silence.

"So nobody'd…nobody would know, ya know? He did it all for free—didn't ask for nothing—not a dime. He didn't even say I had to come to church,,,"

Silence.

"I guess he knew I wasn't no praying man, and he knew he wasn't God!"

Amens heard.

"If he cared about you he just cared, that's all."

B. <u>Goodbye, Goodbye</u>…

The funeral procession rolled into view.

"Lord Jesus!—here comes the Saviour!—a woman cried,

clasping her hands together, tears streaming
from her eyes.

Another woman exclaimed, "What's gonna become of us now that he's
gone! …. Lord help HARLEM! ….what are we gonna do!"

I was thinking about how funerals bring out such foolish,
sentimental utterings but though I do read newspapers and periodi-
cals and know full well that no human being is, in fact,
indispensable—
I wondered too.

The crowd moved in a solemn unit forward.

I swear—I saw mashed rats, dogs, and cats, gather together
their poor entrails and spring aside! …to make way
for the heroic corpse.

Oh yes! HARLEM TOOK ANOTHER BREATH TODAY.

I could not stay.

But having partially escorted home the body of a great leader
disgraced and vilified alive and neglected in death,
and having studied and observed the ways of men in power who
too often through emotional and hasty detour
stay their finest hour—I would say that
Adam Clayton Powell, of HARLEM, was
only one of many.

I left New York City. My birthplace. The firstplace known
as home to me. I left it the way I came in
on the morning I was born—with the
rhythm of this great American northern city beating,
beating, beating in my bones.
I left New York this day, to return to Washington, D. C.,
where,   I,   live.

I Never Knew Sistuhs

                    until
3 a.m. this morning
when my body turned against me
slamming its lesson down m throat
sucking away my very breath
squeezing out great globs of sweat

when the medical men broke in
hauling out my protesting, opinionated dumb ass
to this so-called inferior facility
where a white face is rarely seen,
only dark-skinned braided sistuhs
whose looks shook my protesting, opinionated
dumb ass family into raising a ruckus shouting
for transfer to the so-called superior
paleface sicktorium
across the way.

                    until
these ebony sistuhs and their female ebony leader
politely,   firmly drove them out and
and anchored my convulsive blubber on a table
where their bird-like hands unhesitantly,
efficiently scurried all over me in stoppings-up
and stabbings while muttering soft, soothing
words of comfort, encouragement and,
yes, love ...

                until
my eruptions had calmed
and they were all standing over me in
unrattled authority, their eyes so wise, so
knowing, their leading this fine physician of
the human machinery, and human soul,
instructing, assuring me—

I never knew sistuhs,   until

out I came unabused, understood, unrejected,
mind-improved, and alive! ...
at seventy-five.

July 1998

HUMANKIND

Drawing Of The Line

Where shall the line begin that must be drawn?
What will be its quality?
Will it go straight?—or meander off
In search of sounder base.
Will it be leapable?
Will it merge with the dust?
Will it be trustworthy, accountable?
What will it cost?
Maybe it will be free.
Is it feasible?
Who will the artist be?

        Summer 1983

The Showoff

Man, perceiving himself God, behaved as all Gods do:
    with bravado, originality, a bit of pique,
    and a ready cache of judgment; some bad,
    some good.

He entered awesome places,
synthesized major instances,
created his own creatures,
divined his doom.

Then, resting from his labors, he lay to survey
all he had done and ponder
    what more to do.

One day the storms came and blew away the stars;
the seas thrashed and tore the shores;
the earth broke apart, dispatching man's things
    to the whirlwind.

And there he stood. Bare. Vulnerable before the sun,
unlike his God Hero who
laughingly commanded that
all must begin again
    to be undone.

1983

The Underdog Champion

Out of the goodness of my heart I give to you
A little bit of what I've got
To see you through.
I shall caution and advise
And use my good fortune as a guide
To show you how unwise
Is everything you do;
For I have always been
A champion of the underdog.
For a record of the struggling souls
I regularly assist
I submit my good-done list.

However, I notice that this list is getting shorter.
Is the sensible advice I've been giving
Really getting through?

That will never do!

You must be careful, all my dear misfortune-prone masses,
That you don't catch up with me or
Pass me by with any dubious successes,
Else I shall withdraw my compassion
And be through with you.

Trophies

The most ferocious Bull Moose
The most noble Stone Ram
The most desirable Woman
The most stalwart Man—

These are the ones chosen
To receive our top shots
Because the best of the lot must be got!

Polish that bullet!
Oil that bow!
Concoct a syrup in your mouth—Ready?
Let's go!
Stalk the prize gamely
Keep the trail hot
Because the best of the lot must be got!

Be on the lookout
For the one walking proud,
For the one standing notably
Out in the crowd.
Then rein him in
Persuade him in
Use all your might to
Gain on him.

The word will sizzle the wires
All over town—how you
Captured the prize, how you
Brought it down.

1984

If I Had A Sum Comparable

Ah, if I but had a sum comparable
    to the blood that runs amuck

        in acclaim to fear, hate and
        envy;
        through senseless clannish ritual,
        war,
        and through one's private horde of
        enemies stupidly amassed along
        the way

        I'd create a welfare state fit
        to supply a lifetime of dole and
        subsidy
        to all the likes of Croesus

        for in bags of poverty
        they would surely be
        compared to me ...

        if I had a sum comparable.

            1973

Barren Fruit

The tree which bears no fruit is
no less a tree,

It gives shelter; holds forth as hard
in time of storm;

Its branches hug the sun and cradle lovingly
the moonlight.

True, its lonely sighs do land on the wind—
but softly.

They, as often, tiptoe in to steal up on
an uncertain heart:

A heart hard at host in some
wretched residence;

A heart that needs the warmth and
reassurance

Only a fruitless tree, being free,
can give.

1972

The Greatest Show of All

The thirst to make the Bees
equal his disease;
the way his mind contrives
that murderers also be Birds
and all the Fish
invaders of the seas.
The way he runs and hides
from his own explosive fires
then proclaims that Nature's out
to bring him to his knees
makes

the Snakes crawl and the Giraffes
fall down laughing in the grass,
and the Elephants trumpet it to the Cats
who roar it to the Owls
who hoot it to the Ants
who scramble uphill and down
to notify the Eagle who
flys the news all around
to come watch the antics of the
maddened animal
who thinks and talks and plans
to kill the earth.

TRAVELS ABROAD

Dreamflight

The slow rise of dawn
comes to light
on that enviable
isle
and the fog creeps up
to kiss my lips
and I'm once again
a child
in the land of Pooh And Queens
and Kings. and oh
it does seem
that I've escaped
the bonds of
adult blight and
flown into my dreams!

(And oh the one who has led me here
walks alone and bold
with smiling face
and will of steel
honed to make all dreams
jump real
and she's my
very own!)

April 1983
Over England

Rain on a Swan

One swan, all have deserted her
    Rain pellets falling bombarding the lake.
One swan, no *pas de deux* for her
    Swim little swan, find a hiding place.

    The clouds weep a warning
    Few landbound will heed;
    We, armed with powerful technologies,
    Dreading a deluge, fearing mysterious forces;
One swan, empowered by natural resources,
    Disdaining our sad song
    The lake is all she needs.

        May 1983
        Geneva

The Villagers of Mont Blanc

Playing cards in sight of the mountain
  villagers sit bored by spring
  whose blossoms bring
    no lucre.

Amused, they smile when poets come
  to catch the drift of milkwhite mists,
  to match their meager wit against
    the mountain.

Titans of the Lab and military planners come
  to prowl and probe; the villagers play on...
  their trumps held fast within
  the implacable vastness of
    the mountain.

Only the swift swish of steel against the snow
  assures them, a race is on:
  if another one exists...allow it *go!*
  Mountains remain unmiffed by
    small assaults.

Otherwise, the game over, villagers shall quite
  prefer repose beneath the cleansing
  folds of snow and silver waters
  streaking down the great, dark,
  warming bosom of their
    mother mountain.

        May 1983
      Cully Lutre Lausanne
        Switzerland

Ruminations on the Quai du Mont Blanc
(after having listened to French TV
disc jocks, visited in the ALPS, and
viewed the matches at Roland Garros)

Though I'd like to try my hand at all three
And would likely be better than most
I think singing may be easier than skiing and tennis,
Though I'd surely be a menace in tennis and
A tyrant on the slopes. In singing I'd simply
Dilate my throat and thrill myself listening
to the gold tones rolling forth. Some
Would agree with this self-ecstasy
Other would simply walk out, so what!

It's a given in singing only some we can please
And singers need only depend upon these
Whereas, in skiing and tennis what matters is points,
Never mind that you're hated by all.
It's the form in the former, soaring over
Mountains and trees, in the latter it's
How you hit that ball!

In skiing and tennis it's character—engendered
By health, courage, self-discipline, manners
And practice in the great out-of-doors;
Whereas, it goes without saying (and, mind you,
I'm not complaining) singers need
No character at all.

(While writing about such exertive endeavors
 I've really become quite fatigued
 So will lay down this burden of
 Grub Street labor, and (yawn)
 Become the world's greatest champion
 Singer
 In my dreams.)

      26 May 1983
       Geneva

FAMILY

Funk, Junk And Me
(Or, I Want My Kids To Like Me— If Possible)

Oh Me!—what's a middle-aged black mother to do!
    Trying to cope with the change of life and,
GRAND FUNK RAILROAD too!
                                  There goes Philip! He's
            at it again! My son's going crazy and my head's
    in a spin!

                              Look at that hump in his back!
                              See how his middle
                      caves in!

And on top of all this is his head jutting out and wagging like it's
    stuck on a precipitous cliff   and his whole body is twitching
                      and shaking   I swear!—

        I think my boy is having some kind of fit!

      But he says he's dancing. when I try to interrupt he puts me off
    with
"Wait Ma…I gotta go!" But he's not going anywhere except maybe
          mad in one spot   in the middle of my floor!

                            Meanwhile,
    I can't hear PERRY COMO sing that beautiful song   "Ah yes—I know—
how lonely life can be—-the shadows follow me—and the night won't let
    me be—but I—won't let—the evenings get me down—now that
        you're around—me…" No,
                                        I
can't hear PERRY COMO because that GRAND FUNK RAILROAD runs right through
    my house every day!—and it brings SLY, AND THE FAMILY STONE!

                    I think
I came through the RAY CHARLES period intact, and my children of that era
    are now quite sedate—that is, old. But now, my 15-year old
        Philip   whom I call "Beau" because he's
            pretty— he's telling me, "Ma, those white dudes
                got all the soul!

Well—I don't know; but again, I shall have to rearrange my thinking
    to recall: after all, "what's prettier, really."
  than that song called, "Wildflower"...I'd like to know
      and RONNIE DYSON'S
            "One Man Band" tells a well known story
       and i think that's grand,   and

      MARVIN GAYE's "What's Going On"
    should have won highest awards   and
              RARE EARTH is what I call
clean dirt, and GLADYS KNIGHT AND THE PIPS   are
    class performers, there's no denying it   and

    it doesn't disturb my logical mind
              to define
      a BUTTERFLY as IRON,   and
I'm pleased to know
    there are some GRATEFUL DEAD— they
    make me less fearful
    on account of the life I've led,   and

the sounds of WAR
    have never been funkier,   and CURTIS MAYFIELD and RON O'NEAL
              of
              SUPERFLY[19]
    are misunderstood by some
      but not by me and
    they can leave their
  message by my house
  anytime;

So the gist of this is :

19. "That was a real controversial thing at that time... They were talking against drugs."—Julia Barbour, The Potter's House, Washington, D.C. a reading in the 1970's

next time GRAND FUNK RAILROAD
comes roaring through my door
I'm grabbing a guitar
along with my son, Philip
and mama is hopping on board!

For My Son's Admiral

Dear Admiral of the Navy
you've taken my son Philip from me
I'm sure you'll see that
he's truly a beautiful Afro-American boy
just a little over six foot tall
and a little past sweet nineteen.

I'm sure you'll see his dimple
and laugh at the charming things he says
and please paint his aircraft carrier baby pink
with lemon yellow tulips
to cheer him on his Navy blue days

He's well-suited for your position
being born with seaworthy legs
due no doubt to my devotion
to Captain Horatio Hornblower
during my childhood storybook days

But I truly love the sea
and Philip is just like me

His astrological sign is Pisces,
which practically endows him with fins...
you'll see.

Now I'd like to ask you a favor,
now that Philip's done himself so proud
now that my little boy brown's gone Navy
to see the world
and girls
in every port and town.

Philip left his best friends with his little brother
quite a loud but brilliant crowd
There's that Jethro Tull and Edgar Winter
and The Who and guys calling themselves Grass Roots,

Genesis, Black Sabbath, Pink Floyd
They're also hanging around
You should get to know them, too
They made Philip very happy
So, Dear Admiral of the Navy,
          may I send them all to you?

Jesse's Poem
(For His Twenty-Fifth Year)
July 30, 1973, LEO

Oh, WHAT A MORNING THE DAY YOU WERE BORN!
 THE DAWN CAME UP LIKE IT NEVER HAD BEFORE. IT WAS THE
FIRST TIME I'D SEEN THE SUN, THE SKY, THE GRASS WAS
 EVEN NEW TO ME, AND ALL THE SIGHTS THAT I COULD
SEE WERE TRULY SIGHTS TO SEE!

AND THERE THEY PLACED YOU IN MY ARMS: YOUR EYES WERE
 GREEN- BLUE LIKE THE SEA AND THE HAIR UPON YOUR BABY
HEAD WAS AS FIRE-RED AS THE SUN
AND YOUR TINY FINGERS IN MY HAND ALREADY TOOK COMMAND.
 AND I SAID, WILL BE A WORTHY GUARDIAN FOR SUCH A WORTHY
ONE. THEN YOU, THE NEWEST ARISTOCRAT, GREW
 WITH SUCH A NOBLE WAY AND GRACE THAT IT WAS CLEAR THAT
YOU WERE HERE AS A SPECIAL EDITION FRESH FROM THE FINEST
 DRAWING BOARD OF THE HUMAN RACE.

> (And I was amused that day the white folks at children's
> hospital got you mixed up in their usual mixed up way
> ...Oh My, were they confused! ...they tried to make a
> white boy out of you: they had placed you in their lily-
> white ward on their way to make you their lily-white
> charge, where your lily-white sick tonsils would get
> special lily-white attention and O how they tore their
> hair and went raving wild when I came to claim you as my
> white-looking but (So sorry) very black chile! Then my
> mischief Angel told me to adopt a grand foreign accent. In
> relieved embarrassment the white folks said, "Oh this
> baby is not really colored—can't you hear? ...his Mother
> is part English!)

THEN THE YEARS APASSED AND I WATCHED YOUR EYES GROW SAD
 AS HARD TIMES CAME TO BE NOT AN INFREQUENT GUEST,
CHANGES, CHANGES ALL THE TIME, IT SEEMED WE'D NEVER COME
 TO REST...AND I WATCHED YOU, AND MY INSIDES WOULD FAIRLY
FLOOD AS MY HEART BECAME A NIAGARA OF TEARS, AND I

SAW THE LOOK OF STONE SET IN YOU, MY SON…AND THE TEARS TOOK SECOND PLACE TO FEAR…

Now that you're in your 25th year, pay light attention to the words above but heed hardest the words I've
    left unsaid—for you are my favorite son—
as indeed is every one of your brothers,
as every one of your sisters a favorite daughter. For each one of you is different and best in his or her
    own way from the rest, and in that way each of you is to your loving mother
                   VERY DEARLY SPECIAL

                        1973

To Veronica

Small brown girl.
    Strange to your grandma/ma
You, with your imbued Africanness
Will you indeed see Africa?
And with the dust of my feet walk that coveted,
    honored ground?
And sing new lullabys to my third blood?
And through you will my blood again become
    impeccable?
And my pen cleansed of white ink
    writing vague, half-crazed
    paragraphs?

Small brown girl.
    Already you take pains
To mend our ways in ways
Your dead Grandpa/pa would gratefully approve.
May he and I yet walk with you
    Small brow girl

And our third blood:
    A ghostly but respectful and repentant pair
Through the grandeur of our missed
    munificent
    Land.

1973

Alongside Jeela

Yesterday, Jeela was a light-hearted child
whose smiles began deep inside then
widened, warming the environs of
her home. Happily hand-in-hand we
walked to first grade, second, third
and on...

Teachers and professors were charmed
by my pretty little smiling brown girl.

Today we stroll down the Champs Elysees,
lunch in Paris cafes, climb the Alps,
dine in London Town.

In recognition, waiters bow to her,
Concierges defer to her, traveling
executives harken her every word. And
I lean on Jeela's arm—mostly silent
alongside my beautiful tall brown girl
whose smiles are now dazzling facial
arrangements[20] designed to warm her
corporate world.

20 May 1983
Paris

---

20. Only because, Ma, we stayed up all night talking and didn't get any sleep. I was groggy!—Jeela, aka Jamilla

Sisterhood

Some things are irrevocably true—
    like

perhaps you all don't love me,
But I love all of you,   And

    let's see:

Julie's married and happy with her spouse,
Marsha seems happiest being "spouse without"
Jamilla likes throes of indecision
        like

'I definitely want to be married
but 'ah doan wanna be wid'im'

To Carolyn life is a toss up
an ongoing tingle
She'll be the first to discover how
  to be blissfully married
while staying
  delightfully single.

Jennifer will marry anyone of sound body
  slow mind, large bank account
    one Mercedes, one Jaguar
    one Bergdorf and one
    Neiman Marcus limitless

account, slow mind
big bank account,
slow mind, great art collection,
priceless jewels, slow mind
big bank account...
one yacht, slow mind
    like
We have 7 brothers, 10 sons, 7 grandsons
3 fathers, 3 husbands dead and alive and all MALE besides...

Yes, some things are irrevocably true...
    like
We will always be girls
no matter what we say, do or whom
we're married to...
And, as such, we will always need one another...
So should take pains to be nice, sweet and loving
always, to each other....to last through
the days when we'll be older, uglier, alone—
    and no one is ringing the phone....

Yes, some things are irrevocably true, my dear ones,

Some day you will need HER
And
She
Will need YOU.

1989

Apologies to Mother on her Birthday[21]

February 3, 1972

Copyright © 1972-2012 Jamilla Rhines Lankford
All rights reserved

Yes, we know you're right
and we have been all wrong.
Because we are contrite,
we wrote this birthday poem.

We're sorry when we're hasty,
repentant when we're slow
and absolutely mortified
about what we do not know.

We know we've been ungrateful,
and made your life a wreck
and owe you for the air we breathe.
Will you take a check?

---

21. "I'm the mother of a lot of people. At least they're going around the United States saying they're mine. I just hope they conduct themselves accordingly…this Christmas they did something I didn't like too much and so they said, 'Oh, Mother, well we're going to make it up to you on your birthday' and they called each other from Seattle to California to Yale and all across the country… 'What about Mother…she's angry with us'. So, anyway, come my birthday, February 3rd, there my oldest daughter comes and says 'Mom, this is for you' and gives me two envelopes. In one of the envelopes was this poem. I've got to share it with you." [After reading: "I thought that was darling… (lifts other envelope) And they gave me this check. I accept and forgive them for everything."]." —Julia Barbour, The Potter's House, Washington, D.C. a reading in the 1970's

The Ones Who Wait To Watch The Plane Rise[22]

The ones who wait to watch the plane rise
  Are the ones whose hearts will break
A thousand times.

The ones who wait to watch the plane lift
  Will never see the end of it.
Time hugs those who come, kiss,
  Wave goodbye, buy the
Insurance, then,
  Are gone,
But looks askance at them who
  Wait to watch the plane.

The ones who wait to watch the plane depart
  Hold a collage of dreams within
Their hearts; have weaved them gold
  When they were rust, have
Charted an arduous course,
  Have placed a leaden
Tiara upon the head of him
  Or her within
The plane.

The ones who wait to watch the plane ascend
  Will never mend their ways—oh no,
They'll explore as long as
  A filament of precious gem is
Suspect, and when discovering none
  Will explore, explore,
And explore again.

22. "If you've got kids, and I've got 12 of them…, you can believe I've been to every airport in the country to see one or the other off on some kind of errand—of mercy…or revolution—and it just breaks my heart. They all think I'm crazy. I go to the airport. 'Mother, I've got to go to California.' 'Well, wait for me. I'll join you at the airport.' When I got there she had left. I think that is mean. 'The plane left.' 'Well, you knew I would be there.' Anyway, I wrote this poem."—Julia Barbour, The Potter's House, Washington, D.C. a reading in the 1970's

Are they, lovesopped?—duty-logged?
  Glory-struck?   Martyred?
Perhaps all apply; but
  Shepherds of the human flock, I
Call them who wait
  To watch
The last lights
  Dimming
In the
  Sky.

1975

Tired Old Words
(To my children)

I wish I could think of some
Memorable words to say
But all I can think of is
I Love You,

I wish I could spin some
Witty phrase from my brain but
All that comes through is
I Love You.

As this mother grows old and slow
And creaky
My brain sloshes like soup
And is twice as weaky
And try as hard as I might
Nothing substantial comes to light
in my fading mind
Except these tired old words
I Love You—

I don't know why— maybe because
They're true.

AFRICA

African Wildlife

Africa grows impala
   wildebeest
     hippopotami
    lion
     hyena
      crocodile
       elephant
  leopard
  flamingo
        giraffe and many other animals.

Africa does not grow bald eagles
   or bear
       nor is she especially know for dragons.

The Poets of Africa

I surmise why Africans might be the most sensuous poets in all the
      world.   Their land commands it so. Its rhyme
                                  is the time
                        of day and night
               day and night. .
      And its beauty must be borne in the
    African mind until the day he departs for
the house of his ancestors.   O

     what remembrances must mesmerize the African!
       What dazzling tapestries lie in his sight and
envelope him in the lush mystery of his night-times.   Ah!

                  what Leopards!
         What Kings Lion!
                          And Yea!
   bown down even to Oricous circling circling...
What magnificently authoritarian   Sun-!
    What virginal dewey dawns to gently prod him
from his slumber.

                What
    voluptuous silvered moons   to endow   his wisdomed
soul!   and urge his words to paper   words
  spiraling from the sultry environment of his
               diamond earth

                Words
                      all
  diamond   emerald   and gold   emerald and
gold   All gold...gold.

            While I, sterile poet of man-made
progresses   write of   severe things:
   Newspaper findings...remembrances of lynchings...
  unemployment lines... and the business of skyscrapers...
          remembrances of lynching...unemployment

lines...   and the business of skyscrapers

while I write of
unemployment lines... and the business of skyscrapers,
I write of skyscrapers... of
skyscrapers...
I/write/of/them.

1974

Broken Thread

This land and I are intertwined
   as the air and me.
I cannot escape it. Indeed, did I not help
   make it?

From its soil my heirs have sprung.
From its slavery we—my people and me—have been
   legislated free.

Whether or not it was meant or means to be
   my blood has flowed too far
   and down too deep
   for me to flee.
(And blood does have a way of taking hold.)

Yet long ago I dreamed of Africa
   and wondered whether, if I found my clan, they would
   know me, in my altered state;
   as adulterated I would stand
   before them.

Would they love me, like me?
Would we have mutual understanding?a congruent
   concept of the living way?

Would they truly welcome me—the
   stranger?

I fear I'd be judged unfit, for I could not sit
   quietly baking, womanly-waiting-in-abstract,
   turning from the reality before me.

And the Elders of my tribe being all wise would come
   to know me. They would say, "You do not belong,
   you should go home."

My heart would drip in wounded pride
 but I'd abide and go
sadly.

1973

LOVE

A Poem for Love

The door to love
I closed long ago
and locked it with a key
I need never toss away.

But hold for memory's sake
and just in case
true love
waits once more.

Everyone Wants Something All His Own

Everyone wants something all his own...
    something reliable   unpryable

And instantly recognizable as his
    alone.   That's why   kittens

are fashionable   and kids   (sometimes)
    and dolls.   one's own horse

a dog,   a car   even

a gun.   Things unpossessable   even though familiar
    undermine our aplomb;   like wind,   the rain

a tree   the sun   and the firmament

ever moving   moving   steadily on above, and,

of course,   no one   ever

owns love.

    1976

Fair Warning
to reluctant males

Enter you behind these raging walls of Eve
and pay with us her price in full
not half—not part.

We demand more than a scissor's snip
a needle's nips and tucks,
and beads
and mincing ways.

Where's the blood? There is no art in it.
It simply pours with regularity more than rain.

And your blown bosom— is it rich?
Does it rear and heave, its points taut
with the promise of pasture, and oh

where's the womb?
to house the race,
to produce the commoners and kings, to unleash
the backguard and the fevered chaste
the halt and the rapid minds
the authentic kind, the fakirs.

Hearing no witness to your persecution, I,
squawking carrier of facsimilies, yet do caution
your entry here, into this paradise, where hell began.

Eve's curse overtakes us, early dusts the blush
We grind toward the rut of age no longer *lovely*
in our house[23]

grotestques mainly: eyes unlighted, complexions frayed
eyes frenzied, staring down truth...

what a drab exchange for the likes of you who can so so free
and gay all the way.

---

[23] Theordore Roethke, *I knew a Woman*, ("I knew a woman, lovely in her bones,...") 1958.

Lacking A Partner
Play The Game As One

  A solitary soul

needs none

but its own heart

to chart its course

and fired enough will blaze

the way to some steadfast star

being loath once there

to give the route

to those who stayed

and mocked.

RED LIGHT

First love can stamp the character
and reveal the quality of the heart

Strange how a law-abiding acceleration
on command of a traffic light can detain one's life,
can catch you red-lighted and confronted by
an unwanted memory in the next car! And

there you are! Eye-on
with your turning point That first true
trammeled-and-mangled-by-you-until-it-was-lost love Eye-on

with eyes once
adoring once
mesmerized by your presence Now simply holding Still
remembering sad.

(*O prankster fate! to wear the garb of law and beck disorder*)

How dared I survive the dragulous keelhaul of my heart Eye-on
with eyes accusing and justly contemptuous biding me face
the middling quality of love and devotion I
so generously serve
from the colander of my affections Then

my tenant demon took command compelling me swallow
the deluge in my throat and out of my brackish,
destructively honest and quick lips erupted
a fatuous fawning politeness: *Why, helloooo…uh,*

h-how's the family? Your mother? Your father?

Is/your/brother/still/teaching/at Oh! He's in

Tunis…HOW/INterestig…you, uh look/well…(ahem)

a-little-taller? perhaps? uh, ah OTHERwise…the-theSAME…

The traffic light belatedly, mercifully changed.

1973

Love, Blame Me Not For Disserving Ways

Ah Love!—blame me not for disserving ways.
How could I have known you were soon to die
Or knowing arranged for your sundown days
With planned heartbreak, projected pain and cries.
You touched me lightly; and I, impatient
Fledgling, never stayed to learn your flavour
But leaped to bloom before the sign was sent
And so ill-primed grew, alas! disabled.
How many dreams have you thus laid to waste?
What girls have you stricken with your fever?
What young men have inclined to you in haste?—
That you've besmirched and turned disbelievers.
And so love feeds its insatiable grill
Allowing us freedom to do its will.

1975

Love Memories and Silky Music

Love — ah, yes,
I've been deep in it
Yearned for it, spurned it,
Grew cold and didn't
Deserve it;
Had it wrap itself around me,
Totally possess me,
Hated it, feared it, misunderstood and ruthlessly
Used it, and oh,
Ultimate misery— I've
Lost it too…

But let me near a silky piece of music— Ah,
How I remember it!

I go down deep in my memories
Gather them up and hold them close to me,
Releasing, one by one,
Cozy nights, sweet
Morning breakfasts—the silk of my negligee
Sliding across his manly knee— ummm like pieces of rich
velvet they swirl about me—
(Ah, the precious man…as he holds me,
　holds me…)

So long as memories like these curl through my aging days,
I know that the most glorious thing
That has ever happened to me is
Love.

USA 1990

Love Takes Me

Love gently takes me up
  from the place I'm in,

Whirls
    me in its golden chair to fabled fields
   and leave me there—
to prance around
and gasp with glee at the
   luxuriant treasures revealed to me—

Love takes me up
  from the place I'm in
and gently sets me
down again.

The Race of Love

That woman is love is so
but don't try to be *in* it
cull it craftily for yourself
the better to hold to it

With sex be
parsimonious
stingy as [the grave]
while appearing heated for it
Change your mind much of the time
but be a succubus when you indulge it

Let your love be a reasoned guide to sanity and contentment
Man soon tires of woman perennially primed
for cuddling and satisfaction

Man's a would-be warrior
He is
An Adventurer
He love's the excitement of the chase
A woman who appears hesitant and doubtful
usually wins the race.

Tremors After Love Flown [24]
(Sonnet after a newly-divorced lady)

Ah, loneliness that keeps me company
triumphant pest lodged in my wedding nest
I bid you fly behind my beloved
leaving me to contemplate my ruin
and bathe my pain with recriminations.
I'll fill remembered spots with the murmurs of strangers
and allow them count the hours
and probe the seriousness of my wound
While I trudge through memories of mine own
Out into the light of forgetfulness
And if time fails me I shall cower no more
nor pity myself for love's cruel draught
but reconcile with you, Oh Loneliness,
ever a willing and most
constant spouse.

July, 1975

---

24. I stayed in New Jersey with a woman who was newly-divorced. Her husband took the Jaguar and I felt so sorry for her. Poor thing. She walked around the house in shock. The idea that he'd take the Jaguar. I wrote her a little poem that could be for any newly-divorced woman.

Wry Toast

Well, love is over.
And thank you GOD!
What a fool I was
to count on
shapely knees
and dangerous
curves
all over me
and rely on
skin
sweet and
smooth
when in my head
only air
blew
through.

1982

NATURE

A Mistake in Judgment

I thought I knew the strength of trees
Until I saw a shaft of wheat bend to
And bear the will of a hurricane, and
The tree I thought was strong torn in half
By a lethal lash of lightening.

How could I be so deceived!— to
Misconstrue the strength of trees
Which are otherwise so beauteous and
Hospitable.

And how could I be so naive as to
Preconceive the frailty of wheat when
Its repute is otherwise so substantial

Thus it was from trees and wheat I
Learned how unreliable are appearances.

1974

CAPITAL SPRING [25]

Spring arrived
    seeking shelter

The March lamb shivered
    all along

Blossoms peeked then tucked
    their petals

Poor Robin froze
    before his song

April iced
    over all its glory

May came cowering
    at the door

So winter made
    a tardy exit

Will summer come
    in time for Fall?

Will summer come
    in time for Fall …

1976

---

25. "It's funny weather here (in Washington, D.C.) as everyone knows. It really was bad in 1976 …it looked like summer would never come." —Julia Barbour, The Potter's House, Washington, D.C. a reading in the 1970's

Dominance of the Seasons

April's winds whisk the blossoms from the trees,
Makes them skip around the ground
So newly up from brown to grass, and greening

Paints the scene while sweet fragrances float past
And birds *cheep cheep* with pride in tender wings
Reaching out from nest to sky, and bluing

Bathes the budding earth.

Children prance by
And lovers laugh and cling
Reminding me how youth belongs to Spring

How age bows to it and warms by Summer
How Summers burns to Fall
How Fall give up its gold to the Lord of Winter

Whose might garment chastens all
And whose mood stays, a little, then moves
From ice to thaw, and melting

Rushes down to gold again.

1978

Eclipse

I.   The Assertion

Ever so often I'll block your view,
    My design being to undo your brilliance, and
it shall be done.

Ever so often I'll enter your mansions

and little by little
cut you down to a masterful confrontation with manless me,
    as I lay my breast to yours.

Then breast to breast I'll
splay the splendor of your pinions until
    a persistent rack of my murky friends moves in
  to scissors-down your majestic day

and lay that awesome power you wield
    unto total darkness

For that time/you will be mine.

You shall not overcome/in that place/for

that hour.

II.   The Survival

But I will overcome you in the end.

Your lustrous presence shall bring but a feather's nap
    upon my chest;   your breath, a babe's suck;
Your blot on me, a silken
Throw.

And any of your murky friends presuming rollance
over me shall land in my Gold/Fire stuff,
be cleansed and arise as new as day.

No threat my dear... I,

the Sun

am here.

                February 26, 1979

Fall Leaves

Fall Leaves!—
Beautiful to see
Effulgent by the roadside in stunning
Reds and goldstruck greens.

Purple plus and Russet rouge play
Play in October's breeze.
Of all the seasonal glories
I've seen none to equal these.

All praise too
The plain brown bough
That bears the splendidly dying fruit
That calls the tune for
This Autumn prance,
Allowing this old crowd
A— one last dance
Before new seed springs
To root.

        October 1982

The Huntress

Primed for the hunt, the huntress awaits her game
And is calm, while contemplating its
Thoroughfares and byways.

She has dared show herself—just enough
To prick the prey's vulnerabilities
And become familiar with its
intractable places.

Ah, with what fervor she commits her sight!—
Disdaining swipes at minor vipers.

Meanwhile, she inhales the sweetness of rain
And relishes the beneficence of the sun
Hiding amid the purity of camaraderie
Until the day of stalking comes
And calls her forth, a woman alone,
When time counts down to none.

Noon and Afternoon into Night

I watch the clouds assemble   and stream in imperial pageantry
   across a hot noon's southeastern sky and swell   in puffs
      that heap   until   they spill   frothy mounds of
         opalescent   islands.

I see cloud fluffs   drift off in bunches from the crowd;
   willful   wispy strays   in traceries   of   gauze   and lace

The Sky Queen   arrayed in blazing gold   directs   this   show
   as usual   until afternoon bids her   recede from sight
      her reign ended   on   this   side
   of the world.

Undismayed   she summons her gossamer attendants   Languorously
   they come in   and   stretch themselves against
      the cooling sky   in tones of blue
         and gray-pearled rest

The deposed Empress of the clouds   nonetheless resplendent
   in her diminishing might   spreads her lush
      pink and orange   coverlet   and
      gathers   up her court   into the night.

1973

Order in the Jungle

See the lion
he needs no pedigree
his race and status
are never questioned
he just naturally reins
and accepts as proper due
the obeisance
paid him.

And the wolf on rampage
for caribou
I doubt there's ever a row
over who is who
merely if the
caribou is quantitative
and delicious.

And no twist of fate
could ever induce an ape
to stop to fake
like he was human.

And a tiger's a liar
if he claims he's a hyena
and an elephant ain't
an ant
either.

So the crocodile slides its way
and the kangaroo jumps his'n
posing no identity crisis
in the animal kingdom.

All is orderly, you see.
Rather different than
you
and me.

Ordinary Blues

Ordinary is worse than being poor
I'd rather be tawdry
It's like catching cold
Or being named Keith or Audrey.

People are born,
People die
There you are
Here am I
If this sounds like a song called "I Only Have Eyes For You"…
Ordinary

The rain comes
The sleet and
And snow

The sun shines
Flowers grow
The sky is blue
The grass is green
The moon shines down.
See what I mean?
Ordinary

THE COYOTE'S LAMENT
from "Sunday Morning: CBS, September, 1984

Here they come, those mad hunters of television
looking for creatures more photogenic than I.
And there goes the big grizzly,
sure of his star quality,
hogging the camera—
        oh well, I'll just slink on by.

Maybe they'll catch me, passing down by his ankles.
Maybe they'll catch at least the side of my eye.
Look at that hulk posing!
Being cutesy for the cameras.
Ugh! Look at Kuralt—
                and that worshipful smile

It's disgusting how he goes for the bulk and the beauty
of untamed creatures caring naught for their brains;
which, in any case, would preclude
the big grizzly who
when not jumping *Donder and Blitzen*—
                just stares into space.

But the world of television is all
sex, glitter and glamour.
For its capricious attention I'll neither
pose nor beg.
I'll be logical; and realistic—
                as usual,

For who *could* care about
a lowly Coyote
sneaking around,
head hanging down,
undistinguished in feature, his tail—
                      between his legs.

1984

The Natural Circumstance of Glory

If we did not look with love on splendor
    how could we adore the sun
    or rear rapacious after its beneficences?

In the night the moon lavishes its luminous dew
    on the hearts of lovers
And O how lovers drench themselves in balm
    from this matchless jewel.

If we did not look with love on splendor
    how could we be so moved?

That nature's spew is nonpenurious intrigues and
    weighs upon the mind.
Mystified we stand before the grandiose swell of earth
    to mountain rise;

    its inchdown to valley,
    its laziness expressed in stretch of arid plain,
    its floods that seize our domiciles, then recede
        to flood
    again, again ...

We gaze in awe and ponder what makes the seasons move;
And pine for spring and never mind that April's month
    is cruel.[26]

The way we wrest the earth's effect and preen and
    lean to pomp
Is in accord with the natural circumstance of glory,
    is not odd...

If we did not look with love on splendor
    how could we adore and
    praise God.

---

26. T. S. Eliot, *The Waste Land*, Section I, 1st verse: "*April is the cruelest month...*"

They Still Write of Snow and Rain

    They still write of snow and rain…
and weeds,
    and morning and evening,
and plains,
and trees and marshlands,
and winds,
and seasons and seas,
and of clouds.

    They still write of these as though the settling down
    will undo
the mighty deed,
or at least catapult it
into the jealous and ravenous cavity of
    human understanding.

    But the pounds of floating froth,
the signs of time and tide,
the prima donna air,
the stalwart stalks and phenomenon of
    sucking ground,
the stretched dirt,
the peasant plants,
the specious coverlet of white and the worldly waterfall—
    these, all nature's issue,
while readily bending to pats of panegyric and presumptuous
verbiage,
defy attempts at tempering or
    curbation.

And facsiniacal man, rigged for inquisitiveness,
one-leg prowed in the door of solution,

    fevered
with impatience at poets' views of earth's décor, leave
to explore the non-atmos,
seeking elusive Clown Answer in the peregean/perehelial swatch of
    temptingly hung honeycombs.

And a poem remains germane,
    pulsating through bondage, Diaspora or desolation,
    leaping into each generation blissfully credulous and plump
with each new bard's first sight and feel of
his earth's accouterments.

How relevant then, must be the poem that pursues and grasps the
spirit, holding the life of a man/woman/nation, Stark—

Crammed with eternity's lesson in comedy, tragedy, or
    disdain, or paragon, or
    terrible
    example.

Wild Grass

I like the look of untampered things.
Wild grass,
The sky
A familiar look
In the human eye,
A freshly-born baby
The burst of Spring
The look of faces joined
In community sing,
The fire in the Sun
The wink of Stars
The look of people
Wherever they are,
A tree, standing still,
Any highest mountain,
Any country hill
The look of girls
Being married in June
And the old look of
The moon.

SELF

Everytime I'd Think a Poem

Everything I'd think a poem or play
   I'd run to get a pen but before I'd be halfway through
     I'd have found out
    I was going to have
      a baby.

    So I'd go and have it.

Then my figure would return
  and I'd be complimented on it,
    my husband would re-leer
and I'd feel as proud as a chunk-chested pigeon.

    Then
      that restlessness again;
and I'd start practicing scales attacking any
available piano until my voice would be
"back" and "gorgeous"
and I'd have composed a song to order for it
   but I'd have to forget about it because
     I'd have found out
    I was going to have
      a baby.

    So I'd go and have it.

Then my figure would return
  and I'd be complimented on it,
    my husband would re-leer
and I'd feel proud as a fan-tailed peacock hen.

    Then
      that restlessness again;
and I'd be beautifully read Ophelia
and dance myself sweaty to recordings of Swan Lake
and West Side Story in front of the awed eyes of my children
   and my finally humbled husband.

With my ego now towering like The Eiffel
I'd advance on my best stationery, the Crane,
to advise Katherine Dunham and Martha Graham of my
whereabouts but before I could mail the letters
        I'd have found out
        I was going to have
        a baby.

        So I'd go and have it.

Then my figure would return
    And
I'd be complimented on it. My husband would re-Leer
And I'd feel proud as a
    well!—a Flamingo-marked, Five-foot-ten guinea
  fowl!

        But,
there was that restlessness   again!—By
This time,
    I had begun to say
Massive Hail Mary's
And at the top of my voice shout
    The Act of Contrition
And in the Confessional tell all my personal
  business...

And ask my Confessor, to please pray that I too,
    would soon as possible
      have some rhythm[27] since it was clear
I hadn't gotten any of it
When it was being passed out!
        out!

Then one day
    the labor room
    I needed no longer fear;

---

27. Nickname for the Catholic Church's approved birth control method: avoiding sex during estimated fertile periods.s

Left
   with this extraordinarily new idea
was obviously all I was left with, since
my figure had disappeared, and
my husband's Leers had been re-navigated.
No longer proud I could now
be comfortable: because, my talents too,
   had gone the way of
No More Babies.

Challenges, Set Aside

This day is like all others:
    a Spring one, the end of Summer, one
    drenched with autumn's color or sharp
    from winds iced by Winter's cold.

I've met no one I've had more than three minutes time
    for, as usual
Though I've tried to make each moment as congenial as
    they say I am.

This day is a lazy one for me, which is unusual.

I simply see no need to get involved, be concerned
    or care, or write, or read, or clean the house
    or shop—

I don't even want to go out to get the mail
    and if the phone rings
    I'll just sit and stare and wonder
    who and why they're calling me
    today.

I wish I could do a magic trick and disappear.

Yesterday I watched the shapely contour of my husband's[28]
    hands, in a different way;
    quite apart from anything to do with me
They reflect his personality, after all,
    competent and strong
    when he pleases…

How he'd laugh *hohoho* if he knew
    I was dreaming about those hands of his

Sometimes I wish they were big enough to hide me.

If they were, I'd jump right in,
    until tomorrow.

1972

---

28. Delaware SaCondore Barbour, May 19, 1927-January 26, 2002

The Natural Dancer

Someone always finds my corners—
Only when I'm out
Thrashing through the crowd
Am I alone
And strongest.

It seems
A power billows
From my corners,
Drawing in those who seek
A hearing
Or a companionable assurance
Or who are simply out
To claim a power not
Their own.

I don't begrudge
The intrusion.
My privacy wears Red Shoes
And I, the natural dancer,
Never linger long.

        April, 1985

No One Has Taken Me By The Hand[29]

No one has taken me by the hand,
                up to HARVARD.

I've not even had the prisoner's time to read, meditate—become
            the criminal scholar.

Being not scared,   i've withstood the glares of family   when i've
run off   to a movie,

burned the salad,   scorched a male shirt   shown incompetence at
cleaning the toilet.

When i'd hole-up a day in the library,   i'd   be ostracized
for weeks: my spouse

would repair to the bedchamber,   alone

after his delivery of sobering lectures on my likelihood of becoming
a library whore.

But the family coffer slacking, all was well   i'd be urged to seek
my true worth and identity in

typing—   (sometimes word processing); commended therein for

exquisitely turning out reports and briefs,   my spouse would soon

ferret THE TRUE REASON: my pretty knees.

---

29. *Inspired by the NORTON ANTHOLOGY OF MODERN POETRY account [p. 1252 (1973] of how the poet Gregory Corso, after only six years of schooling and three years of prison, (where he was introduced to the classics) had a "pivotal" meeting with Allen Gins berg, then with Violet Lang who "brought me to Harvard" where fifty students paid for the cost of printing some of his poems. Written in a minute of self-pity, this piece, however, is well unfounded since my daughter Jamie not only gave quite a hand in getting my work to the public but this year gave me a vacation in Europe.*

Now, I. Here. Ancient & staring; children and spouses still crawling through my skull...

methinks i should have been a tub.[30]

Summer 1983

---

30. *Originally, I likened myself to a Rug, titling this piece, "Feeling Walked on". But recalling that carpentry's propensity for flight (a la Alladin), that is, getting the hell out of onerous situations, I thought my analogy quite unsuitable.*

If I Could Rake the Dreams I've Had

If I could rake the dreams I've had
They'd heap so high they'd
crowd the stars, expunge the sun
retire the worn out sky
sink the clouds, fade the rainbow,
douse the moonlight's rays
then when friends have fled
and heirs stayed naught
rain down dreams
to end my days.

Obsequies

If excuses were Nooses I'd have long been hanged:
  my progeny my executioners
  grinning ancestors the courtyard gang
  false comrades my pall bearers
  while old lovers' crocodilian and dirty dirge
  accompanies my botched carcass
  to its single creditable purge.

    1969 (Rev. 1973)

I'm Always Losing Things[31]

Just when it seemed I had the answer to life
    I lost it.
And I had searched so long; an
    interminable time.
With my logician's mind I took up
    sifted, cast about and cast off all
    ages of learning and thought
    then added some of my own.

I know I had the answer to life
    just a moment ago;
Now it's gone.

---

31. Published in *"The Hatchet,"* The George Washington University Campus Newspaper, Arts Supplement, September 17, 1973

In Remembrance Of A Best Friend
(Who I hope is alive and doing fine, somewhere)

Remember you said we'd end our days together? …
You in a hammock and me snug in a swing on the porch of the
Old Folk's home recalling dismissed dreams and
Cracking with laughter over
The bores we've known…
Well, girl-buddy; where are you?
I'm about ready
And my mind's filled with tales I can't
Much longer hold.

You knew all the time I'd come to writing poems
Didn't you?
My husband knew too.   But he, albeit lovingly,
Thought me too stupid to do myself justice
Without supervision.

You said I was too.
Well, that's ok—even now I shan't deny it
For in many ways it's true.

But neither of you
Stood by me.
Before I knew it you weren't around to advise
And he had died, long before
My time.
But I've pulled through:
My mean streak saved me.

You remember the guy you said I should ignore?
I married him.
Husband Number Second.
The wreck of that alliance tops the wreck of the
Andria Doria.

And now; what about you?
The last thing I heard you had captured the heart
Of an architecturing wizard—or was it a ball player from
Vera Cruz—
Whomever, I know he was a boy of flawless manner
And irrefutable elegance: the grandee of whatever his profession,
You perfectionist you.

1974

Time

I would stay the time
If time would only stay
But each time I grab a minute
A minute goes away.

When I try to pass the time
I find I'm much too slow
And when I think I'm catching up
Time's already flown.

It seems I'm to never have the time
Since time goes by at will
When time come to bury me
Will it then stand still?
Will it then stand still…

1975

Surrender to the Sun

When in the middle of the sleep
Dreams shake me wake
I rise to give them life
But find my intentions bridled,
My ambitions groping air.

The floor warms to my bare feet.

The sight and sounds of family rights
Easily unseat my Morpheusian triumphs
Even while I implore the Sun,
Standing helpless to constrain
My dreams being carried off by
The steely light of day.

Since the Sun is not my friend
I eagerly await the night
When I shall *lay me down to sleep, to dream*
Again.

1984

PARENTHOOD

Children, Anyone?

Early learning
    is hard begotten.
Trickster youth
    bars entrance in.
Gently trot your charge
    before you.
That he may better show
    his mien.

Be prepared for
    cerebral swelling.
This edema will
    pass in time.
If he's of the stuff
    and fiber
And if you've tended well
    his mind.

And lay all principles
    before him,
That he may sift and choose
    in kind.
They lay light hands
    upon the swaddling
And carefully
    unwind.

In A Clear Glass Bowl

*"Louise Brown…the world's first 'test-tube' baby
was kept in a glass bowl for two-and-a-half days…"*
  Dr, Steptoe, The Washington Post August 12, 1978

Once in a clear glass bowl
there grew a child wild and beautiful.

Ah, there Louise lay fictile
in a bowl of glass
in the clear warming water
only two-and-one-half days from her
  Mom…

  did she miss her?

Louise, unmindful of her dad's great lonely cry
  unleashing her.

  there she lies:

guarded, secure, safely cradled
in crystal.

Ah Louise, take my one last tear.
Arise graceful and cool
And unneeding.
jauntily leading us past the girdles of birth
  and of love…

  I'd be the last to curtail you.

I remember when glass bowls held
only Geraniums.

1982

Play on a Premise

"People who have no children can be hard:
Attain a mail of ice and insolence..."

So wrote the genius black poetess.
  (You may be sure I know my place: it's
  ten paces behind one who writes such
  compelling verse.)

                           But,
People who have children, can be worse.

        Indeed, child-begetting is often a handy ruse
          to offset rumor (or ruinous news):

    I mean, it can be carefully contrived to, among
other despicable reasons— to keep one's heterosexual
image
   live!   (Alas—with motivation so ribald and vicious
       no wonder lovemaking is often only extemporaneously
delicious.)

        In any case, the child (hooray) is born;

            The Rich give him nannies, swiss schools,
    fast cars, taxless projects, hand-carved guitars,
    catered orgies complete with heroin, speed, mari –
                                  juana—
                  <u>everything</u>, except
        Papa and Mama.

The MiddleClass needs be more insidious.
   Hanging on a budget usually precariously balanced on the
   edge of Mount dwindle, are child privileges: not, mind you, from
   normal attrition but because the child endangers family position;
   and, if at sixteen, he is still a threat (and is inclined to give
      vent to his mind) out he or she goes—
or they charge him rent.

The Poor? If the
"Unfortunate" young can become numbed
to family begging and taking care of
younger siblings,
Some may become President,
through there's less for than against it.

Prayer for a Good Motherhood
— in case of a bad marriage, or none at all

Let me catch your childhood this one second, Love!
Hold your perfect time a while;
Stay the flow from your golden era
Just a little longer now.

Too soon I'll see me reincarnate
In your fault
and come to wring my hands in rue
For me and you
And for my poor selection
of the father fount.

Let me begin the storage of your loving ways:
Your baby kindnesses and need of me
My daughters.

The telling way, dear sons, you
Naturally accord me your small protections,
Your tendernesses—
Let me consider them
Blessed.

Let me take a snapshot this very moment, of
Your truth,
Your innocence,
Your trust,
Your true love,
And place them in the safe
That is my heart.

Let this priceless collection all be
Put away
For days of our rage— our shock
Our disappointments:
For the times when your only lifeline may be
In your final understanding,
And mine,
In remembering.

1982

What is Life

I was fifteen and yearning—to be a ballerina/an opera singer/a circus aerialist and a downhill racer. Instead, I was told that there was irrefutable evidence that I was pregnant. Then I went on to grapple the most absorbing challenge of my days, and the question of just what is life...

all i know is   i felt it stir within me...
knew the thing inside to be alive   and
bound to grow

an instinct prodded me somehow to guard
and guide a life that i surmised was   at least
as good as mine

and perhaps if luck   and prayers   and sense
were on my side i could bequeath unto this earth
the breath of a far worthier

survivor

1982

Hasty Conception

Neither stopped to score the darkness
nor did they contemplate the light.

The seed they cast was unbeknownst and so
it sprang from them a queerish sprout
of strictured sight.

Unhomed, it found no place;
no place from fondness gave a nod.

It seemed that even the sun
frowned down daily at this seed's bowlybeg
for some small nth of brightness…

as had God.

ON POETRY

A Laudable Avoidable

Oh, to be the Shakespeare of my time
to tarry, forsooth, not to marry
to better wind my mind
to better tend my personal post
stirring to no signal but my own.

Then to Henry's goodly plot
I'd lend wise assist
in persuading
no lawyer's birth be known.

A Poem for Poetry

> ...I am not yet born; forgive me for the sins that in me
> the world shall commit...rehearse me in the parts I must
> play and the cues I must take when old men lecture me...
> and the beggar refuses my gift and my children curse me...
> I am not yet born: ...Let not the man who is beast or who
> thinks he is God come near me...O fill me with strength
> against those who would make me a cog in a machine, a
> thing with one face, a thing...Otherwise kill me.
>   Louis MacNeice, PRAYER BEFORE BIRTH

For you yet unconvinced of the need for quality improvement of
the human race, or
for complete erasure, I suggest you read MacNeice's
Prayer Before Birth

because, it is a most worthy poem
because, it so aptly describes the kinship of mankind with
the sewer rat
who
might well be found more reputable at that,
given serious attention.

It describes the Archdevil Man really is—
The quintessential *fiend!*

The most fitting paradigm for evil
this old earth needs—everybody's nightmare,
nobody's dream—when you think on it;
and, as drawn by this man MacNeice who having been forced
entry into this foul arena only, I daresay,
tried to clean it up.

Nobody could have written such a piece but a poet— nobody
would have dared

But it's the best case for abortion around today.

Get it— buy it, borrow it, *swipe it!*   Sisters!

Will you spare a dollar twenty-five
for a tear-stained poem? ...   Brothers!

Will it rank your self-proclaimed soul to
take a look...   Hey!

Mr. & Ms. college-fresh, non-down and non-out
of every color.... will it depose
your instructed smear of intellect to buy
a poet's book of life?

>   And if you think MacNeice is a meager, minor rhymester,
>   And Gwendolyn Brooks since the Pulitzer just
>   thinks she's cute,
>   And John Keats was a freak,
>   And Millay a whore
>   And Imamu Amiri Baraka, just another jivetime nigger
>   named LEroy...
>
>   If you think any of this, well

you're entitled
and may be half right but will you also
acknowledge that these poets do not—have not
eschewed the lethal broadsides of life?...
have taken these shattering bolts to their poetic
sensibilities in a singular kind of stride,
with barely a flip-up of an eyelid—
that anybody notices.

But instead of retaliating in mean and meaningless
petty gripes, lies and poorly prepared
underhand tactics and crazy crawling cutting
silences, like

more reasonable, common sense, middle-classified types
are disposed, these poets—and others similar—

like poor kicked dogs, lick their wounds
and thinking of us pick their pencil stumps and
sit down to write it all out—
to warn or rear our souls...to steer us clear, you know,
if possible—

    (I admit that some, in disgust, may not pass up
    a convenient bridge or river; and some
    give in to a gun. But whenever or however
    it's done, it's done to bring
    rather than disturb the peace.)

                                  So:
the day you come upon a poem,
    before you toss it out with the trash or
    put it down for the dog—read it...

    now, in deference to your discriminating tastes, I don't
    expect you to jump enthusiastic over streetcorner or
    bake-off poets...there *are* recognizable great
    names— *Wordsworth, Whitman, Auden, Ferlinghetti,*
Macleish, Derek Walcott, Levertov, Adrienne Rich...

For you, new to the Art, I want only the best.

   (I concede the poem might not be good. Even great
   poets can't write all good poems. You should
   be tolerant. You can't always be at your
   best in the office— you might turn in
   a bad report; or burn dinner,
   or select a bad friend; yell at your
   spouse or children; can't pass
   a test or cheat so you can...)

                                  But read the poem.
If you don't understand it put it away
for the day when your understanding
has caught up with your
experiences, then
take it out and read it
again.

One day courage will pay a call, and *by God!* even in daylight
with you friends looking on you will resolutely step
to the poetry section of a bookstore and buy a book
of poems by Louis MacNeice or if not by him
at least an anthology that has been
de-loused of the self-pitying tripe
that poets can (and do) write—
an anthology exposing only the best love
and concern-guided words for mankind
by the super likes of:

Old mean-man Frost;
   that magnificent worrywart, Langston;
that natural M-A-N, Dickey;
tricky Nikki Giovanni;
even-Stephens, Wallace, that is;
the tragic Federico Garcia Lorca;
the purists Robert Hayden, Howard Nemerov, Claude McKay,
   William Meredith, Dudley Randall, Countee Cullen;
the masterful and fearless Etheridge Knight;
the fearless Kenneths, Fearing, Koch and Patchen—

And by all the others I hope to pay my respect to
in a subsequent poetic scratching
   and maybe someday—who knows?
   could be—I hope so,
one by me.

1974

If I Could Toss A Poem's Words Up

If I could toss a poem's words up
Disharmoniously they would fall
And lest my memory be dependable
There would be no poem at all.
Just a scrambleful of letters
A litter of ideas the wind just blew
Had the poem been so important
Wouldn't the wind have know it too?
Wouldn't the wind have known it too…

1983

IN GROPIUM, AFTER W. S.

O fall upon me, fall upon me ghostie Billy!
                 fall upon me in my

dilemmanation,   my
searchexity   my
dumb atwitter for

the fit word...the consummate phrase...the tale   utmost!

...*You William!*   Prime Englisher!

Ace-Surgeon-of-Human-Souls   KING

of the sniffers
nuzzling 'neath the rank robes of superfools...Tell/ME

          what's new????

  after you.

        1993

O Poet Tell Us, How Many Twists Of Heart How Many Smiles…

("Mrs. Barbour, how many poems have you written?")

What poet can accurately count her poems.
How tally upstarts of joy and persistent sorrows:
"Everything's fine" could sum today,
But what say tomorrow?

How count poems inscribed on lost brown bags
On table napkins—
How count the ones instantaneously sprung
Only to be shunted to some back corner of thought
And there forgot
in deference to interruptions.

For poets are but our undressed souls
Daily, nightly marching before us.
Relentless pickets of our duplicities,
The few proud times—
The shame.

Sparing none
Nor even themselves the entries rife
With ignoble deeds
And those half and finely done, poets over and over
Meticulously enter hateful debits and lying credits
Fighting off in glorious meter maniacal trys
To juxtapose and reconcile
The contradictions of our iniquitous,
Cowardly lives,
And so it goes—the well-kept ledger
of Life.

1974

Poems Landing

Poems come in to the poet like birds
   long in hovering over beaches
   known only to them.

   awaiting the right wind when
   a perfect purview instinctifies
   and guides the
   landing in.

The cerebral stretch, like sand abandoned
   shivers with expectancy
   withstanding the groans
   of poems landing after
   hovering so long.

   But treacherous synapses beckon odes
   struggling—straying
   through the travel night—

Poems among the missing and poems landing
   broken—crippled
   from the beginning
   of flight.

Poser

Have you ever written a poem profound
    prophetic,   and polemic in intent;

symbolic,   timely,   of indisputably
    eruditious bent?

Have you ever written such a poem? ...
    then forgot what it meant.

1973

RACE

Aftermath of a Game

There's a little girl out there,
Combing and brushing my daughter's hair.
She wants to be the hairdresser;
She wants my Susie to sit in the chair.
They're playing, "Beauty Shop."
    Just a game.

The little girl tugs and pulls at Susie's
Blond, curly locks, and laughs
At how the sun gets in "…all your tangled up knots"
And how she's "gonna put that old sun out!"
Because she's "in charge of this beauty shop!"
    Just a game.

Susie, growing restless, complains, "Hey Treena, Ouch!
Let me comb yours some, my head's gettin' sore on top."
"No!" Treena shouts, toucher her own
Tightly curled coop, "Mine doesn't need
combin'. Yours won't stay down,
It needs brushin'
A lot."
    Just a game.

Then, from the door of her house Treena's mother shrieks,
"Treena! Are you crazy! Come in this house!"
Treena turns meek.
But on the porch she calls out, "Susie, I'll be back!"
Treena's mother pulls her through the door
After giving her a slap, and me
A frozen stare. She doesn't care
That we are also black,
And my pain, like hers, has
No end; for I too know the game's
    Unfair.

Where There Are No Strangers

O to walk straight and wide and free, breathing confident
my share of air, where there are no strangers:

> where my welcome would be measured
> not by ostentatious treasure
> nor by what corner of the earth the seed of me
> was first cast in;

> where my sure tread and steady eye
> would suffice to get me by and
> the pleasure of my company would lie by
> the trust I'd inspired therein.

O to walk straight and wide and free, breathing confident
my share of air, where there are no strangers:

> where nobody would care
> about the texture of my hair
> nor be guided by what tint of skin
> I walked around in

> where the aspect of my face
> would provoke no thought of race
> but compel all respect due, just
> because it's human

O to walk straight and wide and free, breathing confident
my share of air, where there are no strangers.

73,000 DAYS TO BREAKTHROUGH[32]

Note: Italicized quotes denote poem titles or phrases, in full or in part.

If ever this poem is read out loud   I pray
a favoring sky works to restrain the clouds   from dampening
the celebration of this a seventy-thousandth day away
from the beginning

And if there is cannon to be fired   let go the thunder!
And if there be fireworks let them divide the air   with spangled fire
spit there and be lavishly applied   otherwise to embellish this hour most memorial

For surely it was not intended   that servitude upon these shores would ever
end in the King's name   but it became

And surely the sweet bell of liberty   rang out for you   when it rang for me
and surely   the bloodied pen scripting   *my* manumission   relieved your own
perdition

Now do I sing a song to dark poets   long dead   entombed in sorrow
power-stifled pride-revoked   I bid them   invigorate
their beat-down moldy bones   and live again   triumphant ghosts!

Enter Spirit of Claude McKay!   Sweeten your acerbic toast
with the sight of the *"TYGER"* at your throat being led away   purring
overstuffed-to-retching with   your blood

And O Mighty Shade of Langston Hughes   sing no more your *"WEARY BLUES"*
While we unaccustomed *do* stumble over budgets and become captives of crime
the shame's no more to us   than to our fair cousins   whose
"JAMESTOWN MISTAKE" bedims all blunders
of yours and mine

---

32. (The Bicentennial). Washington Anthology, ed. Octave Stevenson, THE POET UPSTAIRS, Washington Writers Publishing House, Washington, D.C., 1979, p. 17.

And Gentle Specter of Paul Lawrence Dunbar See our "...*UNSUNG HEROES*"
catapulted to figments of reality   in foreign and native-bones   wars
"*UNSUNG*" before "*UNSUNG*" no more for they valiantly fought armed
with votes   temerity   commitment   and the law
and when waylaid revamped themselves through tearstained days and persisted
in the name of *all* liberty   with arms   from the force   of God

1976 (rev. 1983)

Black Slave Girl's Lament
...Spanning 200 Years

The First Day Of America
I wasn't thinking of Freedom
I was down in the cotton patch
Plucking off Boll Weevils
I was getting strapped
For sassing Mammy in the kitchen
I was on the auction block scared to death
Of Being sold down the Mississippi.

The First Day Of America
Was the last day I saw my little
Sisters and my Brothers
They told me my Master was my daddy
And mean ole black Mammy in the kitchen
Was <u>his</u> <u>real</u> mother!

Well, it's come 200 years from that First Day
And now I'm 21 black and free
I've got a fine job and a fair education
And I ain't proud as I <u>ought</u> to be

I'd like to have a nice black husband
But they say i'm too black for them
It seems like everything's changed
To start all over again.

The master's getting lazy; eats and
Drinks too much, and they say
He carries a knife.
He says we black folks can have all the action
He just wants some fun out of life.

His wife hates him and says he's a sissy
He says he's damn glad to be
Now she's getting involved down the street
At the "Subnormal Poverty-Level Mobility Community Center"
Along with my black brother.

And guess what?
They say they don't want no part of me...
They don't want no part of
<u>Poor me</u>! Lord—
They still don't want no part
Of me!

    1976

Danse Macabre

Slave and Master—Master and Slave!
Remove the shackles—the mark will stay.

Slave and Master—Master and Slave!
Still the lash—its weal remains.

Slave and Master—Master and Slave!
Change the mold—the form is made.

Slave and Master—Master and Slave!
Bound together—Bound forever.

Slave and Master—Master and Slave!
Just for you—this dance be saved.

Slave and Master—Master and Slave!
Whirl together—Whirl forever.

Slave and Master—Master and Slave!
Faster! Faster!—into the grave.

Dies Irae[33]

    Last night I met a husband and wife.
    They were old, they were
    White; feeling death
    And afraid: she
more so than he.

    She said she was nervous
    Couldn't sleep nights
    And cried a lot
    And wondered how she'd survive
if he went first.

    Thus distracted from my original plans
    I said things to comfort her.
    She brightened, and pressed my hand
    Saying she'd like me
to be her friend.

    She was generous with flattering phrases
    Then apologized for the pain inflicted by her race,
    Then invited me by. I accepted, though doubt
    I'll have time to go, but what
color is need, in a face?

    Some say I should have been disgusted
    For she would not have spoken so
    With a firmer grip on life
    Thirty years ago.
I know.

33. *Day of Judgment*

But the road to death is slow
When one is old,
And the signposts of our lives loom
All along the way,
And in the reading, there's often little
to take pride in.

Not many are so lucky as this aged white lady
Who had finally come to know that
Some things seeming fit for life
Just aren't good enough
for dying.

He Died Not In A Slipshod Way
...small consolation,
Dedicated to the Mother Of Fred Hampton

He died not in a slipshod way, legs hard whipping the air,
his breath giving way to a rope round his throat.
His dying was an improvement, I'd say, surpassing
that popular public interruptive shot
which so doles dénouement
to uncrooked daredevil hearts, and so imparts
a quick, erosive look and the idiot's grimace
observed mainly
on the faces
of those
whose heads
have been blown half away. No—
his dying, they say,
was not unlike his birth;
he never knew he died, like
he'd never known he'd been born.

                              Her son died just before
dawn: while the
Army,
Navy,
the Air Force,
the Marines,
the F. B. I.,
the C. I. A., and
the Klan slept

the local law enforcers came—just carrying out orders. O
    they took great pains
  to place those bullets
into his brain.   But he was so asleep
                he never heard
            the smash! of the window pane
          or the sweep
        of hyena feet
as they came scurrying
            like vermin
                    hurrying the deed.

 So after she'd politely seen her couriers to the door
she prodded her mind
to the dying
of this unflinching son.
                         She
  hadn't really known whether his CAUSE
    had been good, useful, or even valid—
  maybe he had been – as some suggested – <u>used</u>,
but his Cause, he took so seriously
  so to him and to her his Cause was
    true.

      And as she thus considered,
    her face, at last,
    cracked its practiced aspect
    and the tears came:

Indeed, they had been held in reserve for
  Just This Day—

    had subleased! as it were, the milk ducts of her
remembering breasts…
    And now, <u>no more</u>   would   the   roughage of
        her mother voice
pamper
his
half-cocked
ear…
No More…need she fear fear's release.

She sank to her knees,
But it wasn't just to pray,
It was to thank God!   for   the   Quality dying   of   her son.

    At least,
he died not in a slipshod way…
he died not in a slipshod way
he died not in a slipshod way

          1973

Perceptions

Reading words writ by those
    whose sole perception of blackness is
    night
I should stand baffled, appalled,
    a stranger outside it all;
    rather,
I feel at home. I read
    as one whose sole perception of whiteness is
    snow.

1984

Song of the New Patriots

Whatever high wave dashed us ashore the skull-stored beach
  this side of Africa is the wave sprayed with the indomitable
    blood of our heritage and we honor the audacity and power
      of its persistence and now stand with arms outstretched to
        receive its full thrash of freedom in the name of our pro-
          genitors who stalwartly bore America's lash and cried not
            over their spilled blood but swore allegiance to this
              ungrateful birthsoil and charged their issue change
                hostile winds to decenter blows for the betterment of
                  humankind and whom, we swear, shall not have hung
                    their lives on Cypress, Pine and Sycamore all in
                      vain nor will they have risked their necks in our
                        behalf unmeritorious, for we will remain fast in
                          their stead and declare ourselves to be the new
                          patriots.

1983

The Advantage

Stockings twisted, half-laced broken shoes, her
  yellowgray hair
         straying
             from under a moth-eaten cap,
hauling a cart on the bus, filled with rags, battered magazines,
    and newspapers
               coat outdated   worn thin, and that
                                         lapped
over
    held together with two big safety pins…

And him—he was given to the mutters,
  cheap neat in a basement shirt, suit and unfashionably thin
     tie
  shoes all wrong but shined and soled so
        that in looking at him   seeing the
    contained
      rage   etched in the stretch of his lips and the glare
        that leaped to the side of his eye
           as you passed by… you <u>knew</u>   looking at him
that
  he
was well acquainted with trying.

But this old woman
And this old man
On separate errands
Were, none/the/less of kind, in mind,
Their ancient eyelids opened and closed evenly—without haste,
like weather-beaten shutters grown tired
of hiding what's behind.
                          Their eyes, so filled with
                bewilderment, disappointment and new
            fright—
        you wondered at
      these two old holders of
        and advantage…
   for whom it had done no good to be white.

1973

I Dreamed of Langston Hughes

I dreamed of Langston Hughes last night
  and in my dream we met for the first time, dead or alive, but
  I thought this an opportune time to ask him about Freedom. I asked,

"Mr. Hughes, I know you know all about Freedom because you wrote,
'Freedom is just frosting on somebody's else's cake—And so must be Till
we learn how to bake.' Have we learned yet Sir?"

    Up here we keep smelling something burning.

But Sir, you also said that, 'Freedom will not come today, this year Nor
ever Through compromise and fear.' Now that in the final analysis is what
I call <u>heavy</u> and what we are about and what I can address myself to… in
other words, that's together!

    I believe you think you know something lady, but at your age,
    you should be able to say it better.

Mr. Hughes—you might know my age, but I don't think you know what Freedom
is…I'm a government worker; have you seen all these young black men with
their fine clothes, beautiful cars?…more than even you ever thought possible.

    You mean the ones with no visible means of support? O I am
    well acquainted with some of these young men…every day
    several pass my way.

And Mr. Hughes you should see all the mixed couples now, I mean down here
in Washington,—white with black and black with white; everyday they're more
in sight and there's not one bit of trouble.

    Lady, I know you mean well but you should know I never used
    dirty words in public. Now you can call <u>mixing</u> Freedom to
    suit yourself. I call it just plain…well, I call it something
    else.

Well, Mr. Hughes, you might as well say what you mean, everyone does these days, it seems; I'm sure you know black people now have big movie star images, and our black girls especially are achieving…they don't have to grow old and alone unrecognized, all they have to do is take off their clothes and be exposed in some of the most prestigious center folds…not only that all of our leaders and educated folks—and you don't need to be educated these days to speak out on television.

   Yes, I admit, everyone's looking at your.

And before you left we were beginning to have some powerful groups going, now we're getting stronger and stronger, doing our own black thing!…now white folks aren't talking about <u>that</u> much.

   Yep, I recall a good old Western song which began, 'I'm headin'
   for the last roundup…'

You're digressing Sir.

   I'm what?

You're getting off the subject, that's what!

   (as to himself)
   Darn this dream!

You must admit we're progressing econmically rapidly.

   umhu…accounts receivable are always meaningful.

We have dress shops, night clubs, liquor stores, record shops…
   I'll admit you are up front. And isn't it a shame…
   General Motors dropped to…ah, $797 million in profits
   for the second quarter of 1973, from its first quarter
   profit of $817 million. Do you all have any input in
   say, the Indianapolis 500?…What about a few ice cream
   stands?…

Why, what do you mean! I don't know what 500 you have in mind but I'll have you know I know all about the 500 Hats of Bartholomew Cubbins, by

Dr. Seuss, I introduced that in my teachers' program for backward children;
And who cares what's happening' in Indianapolis, I just got back from
Bermuda, ans as for General Motors for your information, my aunt just
bought a deuce and a quarter when she got her GS-12 with the loan she got
from her credit union.

> No fooling!…well, well…and—Well.
> Madam. If I hadn't died, you know had I met you
> I'd have made you the model for Jesse B. Semple's
> sister…yes, sir, you would have been perfect…
> I would have called you…let's see…<u>Eusura</u>
> that's right, E-U-S-U-R-A, Eusura Semple, —
> sister of Jesse B.

Mr. Hughs, I'n not only insulted, but confused…and I've tried so hard, for so—long!

> Lady, pass on to another dream please…or wake up
> and keep on reading my poems.

I woke up, crying.

1973

Shaggy Banks[34]

In my dreams I've smelled burning flesh
    heard the screams …
I've braved libraries
And come reeling nauseous from archival rot
I've had to go in hiding to rehearse
Acceptance, and how to forgive
What can never be forgot.
I've had to feign ignorance of my enemies
Pretend rapport with fools
And in countless other ways debase my soul.
Therefore allow, if I now and then depart
To set my scrawl to dews and shaggy banks
In poesy meant to kill a taste for blood.

---

34. Previously published in *Essence Magazine*, Spring 1985.

IN MATURITY

Circle Closing

I see them clean at last
Readier every day.
The hair is combed
The cheek is clear
The pain is giving way.
Position seekers vie for place
So it won't be long
Before they reach
That coveted state
Of them who will soon be gone—
Of them who will soon be gone.

1972

A Scientific Analysis of Sex Offered for the Consideration of Ladies Who Admit to the Age of Fifty
(or whatever age you're having trouble at).

Do not have it at all if you can avoid it.
For admit—Sex at 50 and over (and some say under)
Is not so nifty.
    The Menopause is hardly the pause that refreshes and if
    You're not already through, then you're enduring it.
                                             This you can
tell by your fits of depression, crying spells, paranoia, aches, pains, pills,
  and your Doctor's bills. And about the Doctor's prescribed conditioners
….ladies, <u>really</u>—can much be said about synthetic hormone thrills!

    And, noticed something about your husband recently? …in <u>That</u> state…
      My GAWD! …the man looks utterly obscene,—maybe he's deformed?—

              Anyway, IT doesn't nearly compare with sharing a scrumptious
                Hot Fudge Sundae at Marriott's or Howard Johnson's,
                with a cherished female friend that you've only come
                to appreciate, suddenly.

And imagine what your poor husband's going through: now we know he's
  never been unfaithful to you, and doesn't wish to be…
But the dear man—the Menopause hurts him more than it does you so
      here's something new: Send for a list and pictures of young
    girls, not-as-smart-as-you—who would love a nice home. Need
      I suggest more?
      (Don't ask me how to do it, Ask…your Congressman. This idea
        he'll no doubt adore)
What will happen is: You will still be respected, and will still rule the roost
  (Make this mandatory!): Your children won't suffer embarrassment:
      The family honor will be intact: Your husband's business
        and reputation won't be challenged because he's run-
          ning around on the loose.

Before you recoil in horror, ladies. Consider. While your spouse
is doing exactly as he should according to the Bible, the laws
of marriage and Scouts' Honor, he is in fact doing it to
his Wife, his wife, in your state of mind and et
cetera my dears is, YOU.

1973

Just Passing Through Greatness[35]

I feel an urge to purge my soul of grime
through birth superb, electrifying,
and full of that thing called grit.
I've long known I was of uncommon kind
and it's time the world …whoohoo! …was aware of it

But soft, let me descend from my cloud
for a minute.
Let me examine the cause of my great wit.
Is this genius I feel real?
Or symptomatic of a menopausal fit?

---

35. "I think I'm going to wind it up now with something that may let you know why I am writing all this junk. It may explain my presence here."—Julia Barbour, The Potter's House, Washington, D.C. a reading in the late 1970's

Leap for the Sun

Giving up forty years of hard labor at love
make it a flight to the sun of your life—
an escape, *at last!*—from the vagaries
of youth for which prisons are made.
It's folly not, to heed ambition's spurs
long goading the mind, the heart.
Unwrap your dreams and fly—sloughing off
parasiticals, leaving hostilities aground
while you scramble, climb, leap on top
of your sun going down.

                March 1983

Shining Ways[36]

Last breath is but an intermission
till nature's whim bids us bloom again
and so become attendants in the court
of Kilimanjaro—
of grace and a terrain as bougainvillea
or in some lush orchard dangle happily ripe
or flourish in a tanglebush of sweet berries
or the rush of rivers be
or weep forever the sad and lovely willow
or reside tranquilly
      in the eye of the hurricane.

And we need not look shyly at Lions:
A pride's run could become our daily constitutional.
Yet again we might promenade in human form;
Possessed by human *higher sensibilities—exposed!*

So spit a bit respectfully onto the next dirt
you walk upon—pluck tenderly
the rose.

---

36. Previously published as "We Shall Bloom Again" in *Essence Magazine*, Spring 1985.

The Lifetime Traveler

Standing, looking up at the top of the hill
I didn't know how to start
But I knew that to make such a
Laborious climb
I must cultivate stamina
And heart.

Up, Up, I plodded
Until half-way there I (foolishly)
Thought I saw the end
And the scene was astounding!
And my heart pounded!—
And pounded!
And beauty and youth
Were my best friends
And they helped me climb higher and higher
Heedless
Of warning signs along the way, like
Vanity Gulch
Stupidity Curve and
Superficial Choices'
Dank and gloomy cave.

I often fell in the one
Missed the other
And I set up housekeeping in the third
Until all scarred and bruised
I reached the top of the hill
Where my shouts of victory
Were all I heard.

And I paused
Trembling in triumph
Made all the sweeter by the pitfalls
I'd left behind
And the revelation that now
I could go *over the hill*
Stepping gracefully, expertly
Down the other side.

1982

The Arrival

A Star winked at me as I went by.
We'd long known the secret
This Star and I.

The Moon came out to shine as bright as day.
I waved my thanks and kept
On my way.

The Trees parted as I neared the Wood.
They knew my errand and knew it was good.
I walked swiftly through their promenade
Feeling honored to have such
Majestic bodyguard.

My friend the Wind kept pace this time.
We argued in usual affectionate style.
We knew who was most free
But could never decide
Who was most restless, It
Or I.

The Grass grew a special carpet thick.
The Hills lent Mercury's wings to my feet.
The Sky in sentiment let fall a tear or two.
I threw a kiss, admonishing, "Now, now—
That will do."

Then I saw the Sea.

The Waves rose as one to welcome me.
I grinned at my friends above, below,
All around and behind.
My journey was done.
I had, at last, arrived.

1973

WE SHALL BLOOM AGAIN

We shall bloom again and reign anew
As a majestic Kilimanjaro or
Splendidly grace some terrain as bougainvillea
Or Azalea or
In some lush orchard dangle happily ripe, or
Flourish in a tanglebush of wild berries, or
The rush of rivers be, or
Weep forever as the sad and lovely willow
Or abide in dignity, the quiet in the eye of
The hurricane.
And we should not look slyly at Lions, for
A Pride's Run could become
Our daily constitutional.
Yet again we might be woman and man—
Possessed
By higher sensibilities—Exposed; therefore,
Spit a bit respectfully onto the next dirt
You walk upon—
Pluck tenderly the rose.

1974

INSPIRED BY OTHER ARTISTS

A Pique at Ogden Nash
(written after reading his poem, "The Seven Spiritual Ages
of Mrs. Marmaduke Moore" and before the death of Mr. Nash)

Oh it gives me a rash

to read of a woman so ignobly disposed of

as Mrs. Marmaduke Moore was

by that irreverent Ogden Nash.

I think Mr. Nash was jealous—Mrs. Moore had an enviable way.

Why, what man could begin at an innocent,

sweet, feminine and tender age of twenty

Be installed in marital high society orgy;

Be deserted by thirty;

Accede to urges at forty;

Become adept at fifty

with languages, golf and yogi:

Then go on to become a sage in old age

capable, mind you, at one, "joyous whoop,"

of becoming immersed in the Oxford Group??

All of this, says Mr. Nash, is because Mrs. Moore was badly sexed.

What a thing to say about a lady!

Thus he soothes himself:

Slyly giving unhappy ladies poetic hell.

Badly sexed—Indeed!

Mrs. Marmaduke Moore managed Sex exceeding swell.

1990

Keats Saw the Leaves[37]

Keats saw the leaves as I do, come Autumn.
Bitter not must I allow the thought
Of my pen caught in mid-air
The call of the rump roast freezing it there.
Keats saw the leaves as I do!
And closed out the sounds of Spring and
The overheated songs of Summer,
And noted the red-breast's last whistle and
The twittering of the swallows' last goodbye;
And made room for the glorious drench of Fall.
O sweetest comfort! Keats saw the leaves as I do,
    all along.

---

37. No factual basis here. In his poem *"To Autumn"* Keats never mentioned the turning of the leaves, probably because nature has deprived England of this lorious Autumn phenomenon. In our part of the world, as the esters withdraw, the sun enters to paint the leaves in vivid reds, lush purples and misty rainbow tints. I simply took a loving liberty with the great ode to indicate what I think would have the poet's passion had he seen the leaves of the Washington, D.C., area in the Fall.— Julia Barbour

Night Pleasures From A Stranger
(For Walter MacDonald, For His Poem, "Spending The Night Near Matador")

Today I stopped to browse at a newsshop nearby, saw a single copy of the *Beloit Poetry Journal, Winter 1984-85*, started to flip the pages but was stopped by page five.

Now, everyone knows a dead battery is nothing to write home about, unless you're asking for help; so, though your first line, *"Deep in the game preserve, night coming on, ..."* made my pulse quicken, it stalled at, *"...I sit in the car cursing a battery..."* but, by rote,

my eye traveled on, catching up with, *"...that crawled out here to die. Did it think to find dignity dying far from its kind, ..."* and with that your battery cam alive. And I was rejuvenated. *Oh My!—My, My!* I closed the book.

I like to take poems of fine promise in doses—a line or stanza at a time—for savor, like great ice cream or Swiss Chocolates. So as i did my treasure of delicacies rather covertly bought one day in Paris, at a charcuterie, on the *Rue Du Bao*, I hungrily clutched this last copy of the Journal to me all the way to the counter and paid is price.

Usually, I wait until the crowd thins; this time i braved the flurry of rush hour to hurry home to feed my soul on the promised richness of your poem.
But on the metro I preempted my private pleasure, couldn't

resist taking peeks—taking sips of your imagery in the *"Thousands Of mesquite trees..."* that *"...do nothing but stand around pretending to be flamingoes..."* and how you dismissed their arrogance because, *"All day long they did nothing but scratch themselves, jerking about in the wind."*

Further down you intimate your hunger that night and how you would have cooked the *"Dove breasts..."* you had iced down in plastic bags, had the car lighter been working; since it was not, you would have eaten, *"...then raw..."* but you needed them, *"...to buy off wolves tonight."* –Ah!

If I exult too much, it's only because I'm more accustomed to sentences dressed to kill delight.

I hope I remember to set the alarm—I expect to fall asleep quite late tonight.

April, 1985

Not That You Would Give A Damn *Robert Frost*
A borrowed interest, from the first two
stanzas of "Acquaintance With The Night"

Not that you would give a damn!—Robert Frost
—though I might be paying you an injustice. I've not
read all your works, its true but, after all, you *did*
live as white, so must understand why you can't be
trusted, even dead!...by one who lives as black—

as I said—not that you would give a damn, but I too
        "*...have been one acquainted with the night*
        "*...have walked out in rain...*"   Indeed,
        I've been evicted in a thunderstorm!

And in your night   did you meet beasts there?
Probably not. For in all likelihood you *were* one
So drew the night comfortably around you.

And in my nights... (Oh, how I wish there had never been!)
I wish   my beasts   had stayed away.   Being NO MATCH I
nonetheless   MATCHED   them   (I somehow kept my wits)

And my beasts   I learned   by heart: I parried,   teased,
    challenged   and gave ground to   while keeping my screams muffled
    and at a minimum).

Putting on joys, strutting my letdowns   until reels of revealing
    daylight made my beasts   of my nights   wearied of the rounds
    so proceed to slink away   leaving pain at play   hard
    upon my sunken doorstep YES. I   TOO,

"*...have been one acquainted with the night,*" and
"*...have looked down the...*" MURDEROUS   rather than
"*...the saddest city lane,*" have WATCHED   rather than
"*...passed by the watchman on his beat*
 And dropped my eyes...*" UNABLE   rather than
"*...unwilling to explain.*"

And from there I departed, Robert Frost.

I went my own way   straight into and finally past   the horror of
    day and night   unnoticeably scathed.   But somewhere…
even as I neared the end   I heard a voice   and took a turn
"Alas!   Alas!" for better or for worse   here I come
again!

1990

On Meeting a Great Poet[38]

The poet is powerful, proud he is   and so swelled with prejudices toward my kind
he could not allow me simple felicitations.

Having sent myself quasi-sumptuous and gratuitous
into the realm of his icy aura   I brought forth the best I knew
in gush   and manners.

All I needed was taffeta and a change of color.

His baby chicken hawk wife stood by   favoring first left foot   then right
nervously guarding her   provisions

The poet drew aside his sheep-lined rugged,
a brooding cloak of aloofness   his rooting jelling eye fastened in a
grudging corner of bare acknowledgement

O, imposing One, I thought, like a hound dog feverish on a fresh
warm track   innards jerking   eager for the catch
I have snuffed you out,
have invaded your darkness

O, Great Poet, I tell you I have seen those eyes
non-poeting   somewhere… everywhere before,
glistening in the night   mob wild.
I've heard those size nines   stalking through grass   stealing out,
picking their way down back to exact their prerogative.

38. "I actually met this poet. I'm not going to identify him, but I will say it's a male."Julia Watson Barbour, The Potter's House, Washington, D.C. the 1970's.

I defer to your lack of hand   and think how poems can denote
mixtures of peevishnesses   mini-gripes and knee-taught dislikes
that cling from cradle to grave,
gnawing on the intelligence   long after the acne's faded.

Stevie's Eyes
To Stevie Wonder

Some people have sight   but they never see
how lovely   is a natural-blooming love   for humanity; these men and
woman

        only have eyes
on the outside   they only have
     outside eyes.

Some people wander wildly through the dark of misunderstanding
   aspiring only to
adorn themselves   never giving a hand in
compassion and love   for their brothers, absent a dutiful comit/ment
   to their sis/ters   or even to their mo/thers
and if their fathers   in society   have failed to rise,
then their fathers   these folk   secretly de-spise.

                                           But God
dispatched a WonderBoy to disseminate His Sunshine—   A child
   to shine a searchlight   into every heart gone cold—   Instead
of supplying this child   with orbs of ordinary vi/sion—   God
   flipped the light   to shine backward   through his soul!—   Stevie

only has eyes blind   on the

  outside   Stevie has   In-

side eyes   Inside eyes   Stevie has   has

  Inside eyes...   Oh,

Stevie's eyes   are a mighty beacon,   I pray   that God
   won't   ever weaken   Stevie's Eyes   Stevie's

Eyes   Stevie's EYES   Stevie's   MIGHTY/Eyes...

Ohu-Ohu-Ohu-Aohua... yea   yea   yea...

1973

The Eye of Andrew Wyeth

Impressions[39]

I

ANNA KUERNER, 1971
THE KUERNERS, 1971

"I'm never struck by that stuff—could formations"
        (Andrew Wyeth, An Interview: Richard Meryman, 1965)

Wyeth has no time for sky:

> gazing into the cluttered countenance of Karl Kuerner and his maddened
> Anna, "Why" poses no enigma
> for long.
>
> Anna—
>   the snowy tint of the sun   reaching timidly   inside her window   to warm cold sills   daring to brush its white light
>   against ancient pink petalled   walls, white sills   pink and
>   white sun   and snow patches   on rolling brown   hills
>   forming   a backdrop   overcome by
>   the sight of her
>
>   Anna—
>   a thin crops   of   wild gray hair   in indifferent array
>   Her head   tilted in disdain   mouth wrenched   downward
>   in wrinkled pout   betokening a defiant
>   looseheadedness…
>
>   "I *would*   run   away"   the portrait whispers….

---

39. poet's impressions from : Corn, Wanda M., *The Art of Andrew Wyeth*, New York Graphic Society, Ltd., Greenwhich, Connecticut, 1973

            "But where   where   over that wide   wet   grass
                 would I go?

                            The Eagles   might chase me… Better to
       set my mind   free   at least   and let   ole Andy
                 paint me."

                            Her alternatives?
                            None—
                            Married to him,
                            Karl,
                            Killer of Americans
                            and Deer.
                            But Anna Has
                            clearly
                            escaped him.

                                   II

                         YOUNG BUCK, 1945
                           KARL, 1948
                       THE KUERNERS, 1971
                         KARL'S ROOM, 1954

"I've seen /Karl/ slaughtering the animals…. He can be brutal and senti-
mental. He's very cruel you know….He didn't like the portrait…He
wanted snowdrops behind him…"
              (A Visit to Wyeth County: Brian O'Doherty, 1965)

Karl—
        his gun a child beside him   The perfectionist murderer
              cherishing the   war excuse   and the theory of   the
        hunting class as   regal license   denoting *good enough*

            Karl—
                    failing   to make invisible   his violence   before this
            neighbor artist   who enters   uninvited   the
                        dungeon of   his face…   this artist

    relentlessly seeking   A Javert   armed with
  dry brush and tempera stalking   the
     savagery   of the scene

          III

THE STANCHIONS, 1967   TOLL ROPE, 2951
DILL HUEY FARM, 1941   OPEN AND CLOSED, 1964
THE PEAVEY, 1965   THE REVENANT, 1949

"...artists today are caricaturing the truth, and life to is more serious than that...also, I detest the sweetness I see so much in realistic painting." (Andrew Wyeth, An Interview: Richard Meryman, 1965)

Wyeth—
    himself blended into the tension of his brown shadows
  Crouched beneath each stark bough Himself the watchman seated
    in seething brown corners Himself the pained
    presence meek behind each mysterious   door The
    sudden apprehensive portraiture of purity dismayed
      and sin tucked in

Wyeth—
    painter almighty Fretful in the hauteur of the artist's loft
 He absorbs the vitals of common community until compelled
     attend his voracious easel   He approaches once twice
 again and again then as in a fit of fever   empties
   the soul of every scene onto superb fearlessly truthful
    panels releasing the turbulence the menace in
     common things

     In the slim periphery of Chadds Ford and Cushing
 who'd think to find perniciousness forbearance or
   even joy enough for art

    But Wyeth knows that only fools

     need to go abroad to learn the world

         Palsied limbs   and lives   drag the same   whatever locale or
            station   and surely   sighs of   humankind alone or lonely echo
                likewise   in   Paris   Rome   London   And in the
            kitchens   of   Maine
                 and Pennsylvania   and

                  No Child
                     need own   a   field   to dream

                                      Wyeth has no time for sky:

                He remains oblivious of   lodger clouds   the permanent
          tenancy   of   star   moon   sun   which move
                             merely   to patterns   of samenitude
                                  impervious   to
                                          the rampaging mind of
                man

                             1982

The Feeders

*If it wasn't for the Poor Man, Mr. Rich Man,
what would you do...*   Bessie Smith[40]

The poor went down to see the rich one day,
To hang around in their impoverished way.
An innocent inquired into the embarrassment
Of the situation: "Ah, we don't mind," the
Poor replied, "Indeed, a small charity it is;
The rich require constant inspiration."

---

40. Song: *Poor Man's Blues*, Album: "Empty Bed Blues", Singer: Bessie Smith

The Wit and Manners of Mrs. Alice Roosevelt Longworth

When you're Alice Roosevelt Longworth
You involuntarily mind your manners
Why when you were three at your nurse's knee
You learned that manners are better.

When you're Alice Roosevelt Longworth
and people come round you who do not have manners
You don't call attention to such deficiency
Which clearly shows that you have them.

When you're Alice Roosevelt Longworth
Your daddy was Theodore Roosevelt, President of the United States
and your daddy, the President, invited Booker T. Washington
To the White House for a luncheon date

Which was not only a memorable occasion
But so highly mannerly it indicates
That when you're Teddy Roosevelt's daughter
You'd mind your manners even if you were colored.

And, if you were other than Teddy Roosevelt's daughter
I'd take that last line back
But since you're Alice Roosevelt Longworth
You will, I hope, just smile

For you're known to keep up with the times while minding your manners,
so would be more inclined
to simply correct me on mine, to wit:
"My dear woman, I'd mind my manners even if I were black."

To Countee Cullen

Yet I do marvel at this curious thing:
To make a poet black, and big him to sing!
                              Countee Cullen

For you Countee Cullen no crude pen
Wandered in crippling whine
But sang with a beauty uniquely pure
And equal to the time.
And for that, with no less power
Caught the awful brute
In damming posture
Gorging alien vitals
That spawned a lethal fruit.

So keened your tender pen on sights to blight the soul
So filled with sorrow's ink
Capped by servile joys and legislated wrongs—
I marvel that you dared to sing
I marvel, that you had a song.

September 1977

To Diana Ross

No chinches on you girl!—and all the roaches
   have crawled away.

No rats either!—spying on you from their peepholes
   in the corners,
         and the *Ghetto??*
             Chile!...

As if it ever WAS!

Miss Ross, this is sho'yo' greatday!

(of course now, I amsure that YOU know there
     HAVE/BEEN RUmors that
YOU to yourself, have become very extra,
     extra-ordinary and
Super-Special, AND theysay that YOU are
     affectin' and EX-TRE-ME-LY
haughty stuckUP image   Which is To-tally
incompatible and-doan-fit-in-Nowhere
wi'chall's BLACK ex-PERI-ence ...)

          I Say:

DAMN the black experience! Move it on out Sugar, if it's
   in the way!

Sleek black-satin lady ...
Black princess ...

High priestess of black class …
Your most eminent elegance, MA'am!

(I Curtsy)

Just keep on unwinding your snaky black svelte
   self onto front
     center stage like you do   (Where YOU,
        incidentally,

                O!

        so effectively

   DE-*molished*!

         the Other Two!)

I Love it!

    Yallers-out-of-season-we-got-a-top-
       black banana

DOit! DIANA

To Miss Margaret

> *Traveller take heed for journeys undertaken in the dark of the year. Go in the bright blaze of Autumn's equinox.... I want to tell you what hills are like in October when colors gush down mountainsides and little streams are freighted with a caravan of leaves...*
>
> October Journey, by Margaret Walker

    INTRO.

Miss Walker,
    they tell me you don't like to fly.
    Is that true?
    Well, I don't either yet I do.
    But believe me I sit stiff with fear
    And fully repentant for my sins
    Till the ground flies near.

    THEME.

In nineteen hundred and seventy five I undertook a journey in October, Miss Margaret—Miss Margaret of the "Cypress swamps and muskrat marshes..."

Miss Margaret Walker—Writing your peachtreed, poplar-smelling sweet
    red apple/daoped perfumed poem—That tender beauty—Your lush
        descript saddening out with each upbeat of the train wheels
rolling south—Rolling south—To a land I had never seen—A
    land draw stunning—Leaping real—As your lachrymose pen

    dripping truth—Swings wide to reveal full dress and
    a'quiver—A stricken world's grueling bitter loveliness—
Your unmatchable portraiture—Saddening out—In one long mellifluous
       howl—of speckled black—and white—ecru and brown pain…

CODA.

Ah yes Miss Margaret…
   While you traveled southward, by train, home
   to your "black fields" I undertook a journey in October
   to a school in Granville, Ohio, where
   you too have been known to go—but
   being not so wise as you,
   I flew.

1979

Where Vincent Stood[41]

And there Vincent stood   crying aloud
        and bleeding in the field

    the lopped part
    a sudden misfit flung
    against the vigor of the weeds
        (and preceding its liege by just
        a year or two).

        Would clones have fared better?

I think not, come destiny.   The field
would have seethed a multiplicity—
all trembly
and unhearing.

    Why not a hand Vincent?

    Neither had offended me—it was a
    mood...

And so, his hands—his soul
intact, we're left with the enigma
and miles of glory from

Where Vincent Stood.
        February, 1985

41. Vincent Van Gogh, painter

INDEX OF POEMS

73,000 Days to Breakthrough   212
7th Grade Algebra   65
A Laudable Avoidable   199
A Man of No Account   4
A Mistake in Judgment   162
A Pique at Ogden Nash   240
A Poem for Love   150
A Poem for Poetry   200
A Sad Little Story   50
A Sad Little Story Made Glad   51
A Scientific Analysis of Sex Offered for the Consideration
    of Ladies who Admit to the Age of Fifty   231
A Scientific Condition with God on My Three Sides   45
A Silliness of Politicians and Militants   20
A Time of Dishonor   21
A Vicarious Position Deplored   46
African Wildlife   144
Aftermath of a Game   210
Alien Places   2
Alongside Jeela   136
Apologies to Mother on Her Birthday   139
Ballad of a Stylish Rebel   71
Barren Fruit   120
Black Slave Girl's Lament   214
Bless All The Little Coffee Shops   15
Blood   7
Broken Thread   147
Capital Spring   163
Challenges, Set Aside   180
Children Want Everything They See   25
Children, Anyone?   191
Christmas Bittersweet   9
Circle Closing   230
Colored Studies   63
Danse Macabre   216
Dawnsight   11
Death Wish   47
Deprived, We Adults Grope   12
Dies Irae   217
Diplomatic Topography   24

Dominance of the Seasons   164
Doug's Trouble   54
Drawing of the Line   115
Dreamflight   123
Eclipse   165
Everyone Wants Something All His Own   151
Everytime I'd Think a Poem   177
Expatriate in Harlem   82
Fair Warning   152
Fall Leaves   166
For My Son's Admiral   131
Funk, Junk and Me   128
Go Forth in Preparedness   48
Had My Mother Ruled the Tribe   55
Harvard Yard Blues   56
Hasty Conception   197
He Died Not in a Slipshod Way   219
Humor & Conundrums
I Dreamed of Langston Hughes   225
I Never Knew Sistuhs   112
I Remember New England   60
I'm Always Losing Things   186
If I Could Rake the Dreams I've Had   204
If I Could Toss a Poem's Words Up   204
If I Had A Sum Comparable   119
In a Clear Glass Bowl   192
In Gropium, After W.S.   205
In Remembrance of a Best Friend   187
Inspired By Other Artists
Jesse's Poem   133
Just Passing Through Greatness   233
Keats Saw the Leaves   241
Lacking a Partner, Play the Game as One   153
Leap for the Sun   234
Library Experience   67
Love Memories and Silky Music   156
Love Takes Me Up   157
Love, Blame Me Not for Disserving Ways   155
My Crowd   3
My Father   69
N Street   61
Night Pleasures from a Stranger   242
No One Has Taken Me By the Hand   182

Noon and Afternoon Into Night   168
Not That You Would Give a Damn Robert Frost   244
Now that Man Has Gained The Moon   13
O Poet Tell Us, How Many Twists of Heart How Many Smiles   206
Obsequies   185
Ode to Egomania   10
On Meeting A Great Poet   240
Order in the Jungle   169
Ordinary Blues   170
Paying Dues   14
Perceptions   222
Play on a Premise   193
Play Washington   26
Poems Landing   207
Politics & Revolutions
Poser   208
Prayer for a Good Motherhood   195
Rain on a Swan   124
Red Light   154
Ruminations on the Quai du Mont Blanc   126
Shaggy Banks   228
Shallow Thoughts   16
Shining Ways   235
Sisterhood   137
Some Danced Minuets   75
Song of the New Patriots   223
Stevie's Eyes   248
Summer Song for America   1
Surrender to the Sun   189
The Advantage   224
The Arrival   237
The Assassins   27
The Coyote's Lament   171
The Eye of Andrew Wyeth   249
The Feeders   253
The Greatest Show of All   121
The Half Daft Girl   17
The Heroic People of Prague   28
The Huntress   167
The Lifetime Traveler   238
The Natural Circumstance of Glory   172
The Natural Dancer   181
The Ones Who Wait To Watch The Plane Rise   140

The Poets of Africa   145
The Race of Love   158
The Sentry   32
The Showoff   116
The Solution to All the Problems of Mankind   57
The Underdog Champion   117
The Villagers of Mont Blanc   125
The Wit and Manners of Mrs. Alice Roosevelt Longworth   254
The Womanly Quality   44
They Still Write of Snow And Rain   173
Time   188
Tired Old Words   142
To Countee Cullen   255
To Diana Ross   256
To Miss Margaret   258
To Veronica   135
Tremors After Love Flown   159
Trophies   118
We Shall Bloom Again   236
What is Life   196
Where There Are No Strangers   211
Where Vincent Stood   260
Wild Grass   175
Wrong Gods   80
Wry Toast   160

www.ingramcontent.com/pod-product-compliance
Lightning Source LLC
Chambersburg PA
CBHW032040090426

42744CB00004B/71